CONNECTED MATHEMATICS 3

Frogs, Fleas, and Painted Cubes

Quadratic Functions

Glenda Lappan, Elizabeth Difanis Phillips,
James T. Fey, Susan N. Friel

PEARSON

Boston, Massachusetts • Chandler, Arizona • Glenview, Illinois • Hoboken, New Jersey

Connected Mathematics® was developed at Michigan State University with financial support from the Michigan State University Office of the Provost, Computing and Technology, and the College of Natural Science.

This material is based upon work supported by the National Science Foundation under Grant No. MDR 9150217 and Grant No. ESI 9986372. Opinions expressed are those of the authors and not necessarily those of the Foundation.

As with prior editions of this work, the authors and administration of Michigan State University preserve a tradition of devoting royalties from this publication to support activities sponsored by the MSU Mathematics Education Enrichment Fund.

Acknowledgments appear on page 113, which constitutes an extension of this copyright page.

13-digit ISBN 978-0-13-327449-3
10-digit ISBN 0-13-327449-7
8 9 10 V011 17 16 15

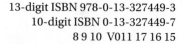

Authors

A Team of Experts

....

Glenda Lappan is a University Distinguished Professor in the Program in Mathematics Education (PRIME) and the Department of Mathematics at Michigan State University. Her research and development interests are in the connected areas of students' learning of mathematics and mathematics teachers' professional growth and change related to the development and enactment of K–12 curriculum materials.

Elizabeth Difanis Phillips is a Senior Academic Specialist in the Program in Mathematics Education (PRIME) and the Department of Mathematics at Michigan State University. She is interested in teaching and learning mathematics for both teachers and students. These interests have led to curriculum and professional development projects at the middle school and high school levels, as well as projects related to the teaching and learning of algebra across the grades.

James T. Fey is a Professor Emeritus at the University of Maryland. His consistent professional interest has been development and research focused on curriculum materials that engage middle and high school students in problem-based collaborative investigations of mathematical ideas and their applications.

Susan N. Friel is a Professor of Mathematics Education in the School of Education at the University of North Carolina at Chapel Hill. Her research interests focus on statistics education for middle-grade students and, more broadly, on teachers' professional development and growth in teaching mathematics K–8.

With... Yvonne Grant and Jacqueline Stewart

Yvonne Grant teaches mathematics at Portland Middle School in Portland, Michigan. Jacqueline Stewart is a recently retired high school teacher of mathematics at Okemos High School in Okemos, Michigan. Both Yvonne and Jacqueline have worked on a variety of activities related to the development, implementation, and professional development of the CMP curriculum since its beginning in 1991.

Development Team

CMP3 Authors

Glenda Lappan, University Distinguished Professor, Michigan State University
Elizabeth Difanis Phillips, Senior Academic Specialist, Michigan State University
James T. Fey, Professor Emeritus, University of Maryland
Susan N. Friel, Professor, University of North Carolina – Chapel Hill

With...

Yvonne Grant, Portland Middle School, Michigan
Jacqueline Stewart, Mathematics Consultant, Mason, Michigan

In Memory of... William M. Fitzgerald, Professor (Deceased), Michigan State University, who made substantial contributions to conceptualizing and creating CMP1.

Administrative Assistant

Michigan State University
Judith Martus Miller

Support Staff

Michigan State University
Undergraduate Assistants:
Bradley Robert Corlett, Carly Fleming, Erin Lucian, Scooter Nowak

Development Assistants

Michigan State University
Graduate Research Assistants:
Richard "Abe" Edwards, Nic Gilbertson, Funda Gonulates, Aladar Horvath, Eun Mi Kim, Kevin Lawrence, Jennifer Nimtz, Joanne Philhower, Sasha Wang

Assessment Team

Maine
Falmouth Public Schools
Falmouth Middle School: Shawn Towle

Michigan
Ann Arbor Public Schools
Tappan Middle School
Anne Marie Nicoll-Turner

Portland Public Schools
Portland Middle School
Holly DeRosia, Yvonne Grant

Traverse City Area Public Schools
Traverse City East Middle School
Jane Porath, Mary Beth Schmitt

Traverse City West Middle School
Jennifer Rundio, Karrie Tufts

Ohio
Clark-Shawnee Local Schools
Rockway Middle School: Jim Mamer

Content Consultants

Michigan State University
Peter Lappan, Professor Emeritus, Department of Mathematics

Normandale Community College
Christopher Danielson, Instructor, Department of Mathematics & Statistics

University of North Carolina – Wilmington
Dargan Frierson, Jr., Professor, Department of Mathematics & Statistics

Student Activities
Michigan State University
Brin Keller, Associate Professor, Department of Mathematics

Consultants

Indiana
Purdue University
Mary Bouck, Mathematics Consultant

Michigan
Oakland Schools
Valerie Mills, Mathematics Education Supervisor
Mathematics Education Consultants: Geraldine Devine, Dana Gosen

Ellen Bacon, Independent Mathematics Consultant

New York
University of Rochester
Jeffrey Choppin, Associate Professor

Ohio
University of Toledo
Debra Johanning, Associate Professor

Pennsylvania
University of Pittsburgh
Margaret Smith, Professor

Texas
University of Texas at Austin
Emma Trevino, Supervisor of Mathematics Programs, The Dana Center

Mathematics for All Consulting
Carmen Whitman, Mathematics Consultant

....

Reviewers

Michigan
Ionia Public Schools
Kathy Dole, Director of Curriculum and Instruction

Grand Valley State University
Lisa Kasmer, Assistant Professor

Portland Public Schools
Teri Keusch, Classroom Teacher

Minnesota
Hopkins School District 270
Michele Luke, Mathematics Coordinator

....

Field Test Sites for CMP3

Michigan
Ann Arbor Public Schools
Tappan Middle School
Anne Marie Nicoll-Turner*

Portland Public Schools
Portland Middle School: Mark Braun, Angela Buckland, Holly DeRosia, Holly Feldpausch, Angela Foote, Yvonne Grant*, Kristin Roberts, Angie Stump, Tammi Wardwell

Traverse City Area Public Schools
Traverse City East Middle School
Ivanka Baic Berkshire, Brenda Dunscombe, Tracie Herzberg, Deb Larimer, Jan Palkowski, Rebecca Perreault, Jane Porath*, Robert Sagan, Mary Beth Schmitt*

Traverse City West Middle School
Pamela Alfieri, Jennifer Rundio, Maria Taplin, Karrie Tufts*

Maine
Falmouth Public Schools
Falmouth Middle School: Sally Bennett, Chris Driscoll, Sara Jones, Shawn Towle*

Minnesota
Minneapolis Public Schools
Jefferson Community School
Leif Carlson*,
Katrina Hayek Munsisoumang*

Ohio
Clark-Shawnee Local Schools
Reid School: Joanne Gilley
Rockway Middle School: Jim Mamer*
Possum School: Tami Thomas

*Indicates a Field Test Site Coordinator

Frogs, Fleas, and Painted Cubes

Quadratic Functions

Introduction to Quadratic Functions 7

Quadratic Expressions 24

Looking Ahead

Suppose you travel to Mars to prospect a precious metal. You can claim any rectangular piece of land you can surround by 20 meters of laser fencing. **How** should you arrange your fencing to enclose the maximum area?

Suppose the circumference of a cross section of a tree is x feet. Is the relationship between the circumference and the area of the cross section linear, quadratic, exponential, or none of these?

A frog jumps straight up. Its height h in feet after t seconds is modeled by the equation $h = -16t^2 + 12t + 0.2$. **What** is the maximum height the frog reaches? **When** does the frog reach this height?

Mathematics is useful for solving practical problems in science, business, engineering, and economics. In earlier Units, you studied problems that could be modeled with linear and exponential functions, and with inverse variation. In this Unit, you will explore quadratic functions. Quadratic functions are found in many interesting situations, such as the height of a basketball thrown into the air, as well as those on the previous page.

Mathematical Highlights

Frogs, Fleas, and Painted Cubes

In *Frogs, Fleas, and Painted Cubes,* you will explore quadratic functions, an important type of nonlinear function.

You will learn how to

- Recognize patterns of change for quadratic relationships

- Write equations for quadratic functions represented in tables, graphs, and problem situations

- Connect quadratic equations to the patterns in tables and graphs of quadratic functions

- Use a quadratic equation to identify the maximum or minimum value, the *x*- and *y*-intercepts, line of symmetry, and other important features of the graph of a quadratic function

- Recognize equivalent quadratic expressions

- Use the Distributive Property to write equivalent quadratic expressions in factored and expanded form

- Use tables, graphs, and equations of quadratic functions to solve problems in a variety of situations from geometry, science, and business

- Compare properties of quadratic, linear, and exponential functions

When you encounter a new problem, it is a good idea to ask yourself questions. In this Unit, you might ask questions such as:

What are the independent and dependent variables?

How can I recognize whether the relationship between the variables is quadratic?

What equation models a quadratic function given in a table, graph, or problem context?

How can I answer questions about the problem situation by studying a table, graph, or equation representing a quadratic function?

Mathematical Practices and Habits of Mind

In the *Connected Mathematics* curriculum you will develop an understanding of important mathematical ideas by solving problems and reflecting on the mathematics involved. Every day, you will use "habits of mind" to make sense of problems and apply what you learn to new situations. Some of these habits are described by the *Common Core State Standards for Mathematical Practices* (MP).

MP1 Make sense of problems and persevere in solving them.

When using mathematics to solve a problem, it helps to think carefully about

- data and other facts you are given and what additional information you need to solve the problem;
- strategies you have used to solve similar problems and whether you could solve a related simpler problem first;
- how you could express the problem with equations, diagrams, or graphs;
- whether your answer makes sense.

MP2 Reason abstractly and quantitatively.

When you are asked to solve a problem, it often helps to

- focus first on the key mathematical ideas;
- check that your answer makes sense in the problem setting;
- use what you know about the problem setting to guide your mathematical reasoning.

MP3 Construct viable arguments and critique the reasoning of others.

When you are asked to explain why a conjecture is correct, you can

- show some examples that fit the claim and explain why they fit;
- show how a new result follows logically from known facts and principles.

When you believe a mathematical claim is incorrect, you can

- show one or more counterexamples—cases that don't fit the claim;
- find steps in the argument that do not follow logically from prior claims.

MP4 Model with mathematics.

When you are asked to solve problems, it often helps to

- think carefully about the numbers or geometric shapes that are the most important factors in the problem, then ask yourself how those factors are related to each other;
- express data and relationships in the problem with tables, graphs, diagrams, or equations, and check your result to see if it makes sense.

MP5 Use appropriate tools strategically.

When working on mathematical questions, you should always

- decide which tools are most helpful for solving the problem and why;
- try a different tool when you get stuck.

MP6 Attend to precision.

In every mathematical exploration or problem-solving task, it is important to

- think carefully about the required accuracy of results; is a number estimate or geometric sketch good enough, or is a precise value or drawing needed?
- report your discoveries with clear and correct mathematical language that can be understood by those to whom you are speaking or writing.

MP7 Look for and make use of structure.

In mathematical explorations and problem solving, it is often helpful to

- look for patterns that show how data points, numbers, or geometric shapes are related to each other;
- use patterns to make predictions.

MP8 Look for and express regularity in repeated reasoning.

When results of a repeated calculation show a pattern, it helps to

- express that pattern as a general rule that can be used in similar cases;
- look for shortcuts that will make the calculation simpler in other cases.

You will use all of the Mathematical Practices in this Unit. Sometimes, when you look at a Problem, it is obvious which practice is most helpful. At other times, you will decide on a practice to use during class explorations and discussions. After completing each Problem, ask yourself:

- What mathematics have I learned by solving this Problem?
- What Mathematical Practices were helpful in learning this mathematics?

1

Introduction to Quadratic Functions

In January of 1848, gold was discovered near Sacramento, California. By the spring of that year, a great gold rush had begun, bringing 500,000 new residents to California.

Throughout history, people have moved to particular areas of the world with the hopes of improving their lives.

- In 1867, prospectors headed to South Africa in search of diamonds.

- From 1860 to 1900, farmers headed to the American prairie where land was free.

- The 1901, Spindletop oil gusher brought drillers by the thousands to eastern Texas.

Prospectors and farmers had to stake claims on the land they wanted to work.

Common Core State Standards

A-SSE.A.1 Interpret expressions that represent a quantity in terms of its context.

A-CED.A.1 Create equations and inequalities in one variable . . .

F-IF.C.7a Graph linear and quadratic functions and show intercepts, maxima, and minima.

Also N-Q.A.1, A-SSE.A.1b, A-CED.A.2, A-REI.D.10, F-IF.B.4, F-IF.B.5, F-IF.C.7, F-IF.C.9, F-BF.A.1

1.1 Staking a Claim
Maximizing Area

Suppose it is the year 2100, and a rare and precious metal has just been discovered on Mars. You and hundreds of other adventurers travel to the planet to stake your claim. You are allowed to claim any rectangular piece of land that can be surrounded by 20 meters of laser fencing. You want to arrange your fencing to enclose the maximum area possible.

> **?** What are the dimensions of a rectangle with the greatest area for a fixed perimeter?

Problem 1.1

A
1. Sketch several rectangles with a perimeter of 20 meters. Include some with small areas and some with large areas. Label the dimensions of each rectangle.

2. Make a table showing the length, width, and area for every rectangle with a perimeter of 20 meters and whole-number side lengths. Describe some patterns that you observe in the table.

3. Make a graph of the data (*length, area*). Describe the shape of the graph.

4. How does the pattern in the table appear in the graph?

B
1. What rectangle dimensions give the greatest possible area? Explain.

2. Suppose the dimensions were not restricted to whole numbers. Would this change your answer? Explain.

A C E Homework starts on page 14.

1.2 Reading Graphs and Tables

The relationship between length and area in Problem 1.1 is a **quadratic function.** Quadratic functions are characterized by their U-shaped graphs, which are called **parabolas.**

In Problem 1.1, the area depends on, or is a function of, the length. Recall that a relationship in which one variable depends on another is a *function*. Because the variable *area* depends on the length, it is called the **dependent variable.** The variable *length* is the **independent variable.**

You have studied other families of functions in earlier Units.

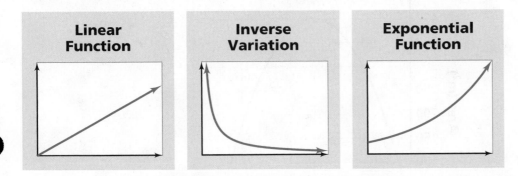

- The distance covered by a van traveling at a constant speed is a function of time. The relationship between time and distance is a linear function.

- The time needed for a van to travel 200 miles is a function of the average speed of the van. The relationship between time and rate is an inverse variation.

- The value of an investment that grows at 4% per year is a function of the number of years. The relationship between the number of years and the value is an exponential function.

You have learned about important characteristics of these functions by studying tables, graphs, and equations that represent them. As you explore quadratic functions in this Unit, look for common patterns in the tables, graphs, and equations. In Problem 1.2, you will look for patterns in graphs and equations of quadratic functions.

Problem 1.2

A The graph shows length and area data for rectangles with a fixed perimeter.

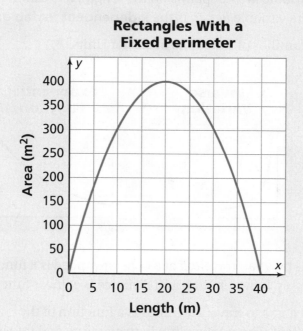

Rectangles With a Fixed Perimeter

1. Describe the shape of the graph and any special features you see.

2. What is the greatest area possible for a rectangle with this perimeter? What are the dimensions of this rectangle?

3. What is the area of the rectangle whose length is 10 meters? What is the area of the rectangle whose length is 30 meters? How are these rectangles related?

4. What are the dimensions of the rectangle with an area of 175 square meters?

5. What is the fixed perimeter for the rectangles represented by the graph? Explain how you found the perimeter.

Problem **1.2** *continued*

B Use the table to answer parts (1)–(5).

**Rectangles With a
Fixed Perimeter**

Length (m)	Area (m²)
0	0
1	11
2	20
3	27
4	32
5	35
6	36
7	35
8	32
9	27
10	20
11	11
12	0

1. What patterns do you observe in the table? Compare these patterns with those you observed in the graph in Question A.

2. What is the fixed perimeter for the rectangles represented by this table? Explain.

3. What is the greatest area possible for a rectangle with this perimeter? What are the dimensions of this rectangle?

4. Estimate the dimensions of a rectangle with this fixed perimeter and an area of 16 square meters.

5. Suppose a rectangle with this perimeter has an area of 35.5 square meters. What are its dimensions?

C Based on Questions A and B, describe the change in area as the length increases by 1. Compare this pattern of change to those for linear and exponential functions and for inverse variation.

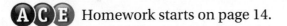 Homework starts on page 14.

1.3 Writing an Equation

You used tables and graphs to represent relationships between length and area for rectangles with fixed perimeters. In this Problem, you will write equations for these functions.

You know that the formula for the area A of a rectangle with length ℓ and width w is $A = \ell w$ and the formula for perimeter P is $P = 2\ell + 2w$.

The rectangle below has a perimeter of 20 meters and a length of ℓ meters.

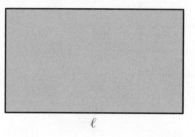

ℓ

> **?** • What equation represents the relationship between length ℓ and area A for a rectangle with a perimeter of 20 meters?
>
> • How can you use the equation to find the maximum area?

Problem 1.3

A Consider rectangles with a perimeter of 60 meters.

1. Sketch a rectangle to represent this situation. Label one side ℓ. Express the width in terms of ℓ.

2. Write an equation for the area A in terms of ℓ.

3. Make a table for your equation. Use your table to estimate the maximum area. What dimensions correspond to this area?

4. Use data from your table to help you sketch a graph of the relationship between length and area.

5. How can you use your graph to find the maximum area possible? How does your graph show the length that corresponds to the maximum area?

Problem **1.3** *continued*

B The equation for the areas of rectangles with a certain fixed perimeter is $A = \ell(35 - \ell)$, where ℓ is the length in meters.

1. Draw a rectangle to represent this situation. Label one dimension ℓ. Label the other dimension in terms of ℓ.

2. Make a table showing the length, width, and area for lengths of 0, 5, 10, 15, 20, 25, 30, and 35 meters. Does this table include the maximum area? Describe any patterns that you see.

3. Describe the graph of this equation.

4. What is the maximum area? What dimensions correspond to this maximum area? Explain.

5. Describe two ways you could find the fixed perimeter. What is the perimeter?

C Suppose you know the perimeter of a rectangle. How can you write an equation for the area in terms of the length of a side?

D Study the graphs, tables, and equations for areas of rectangles with fixed perimeters. Which representation is most useful for finding the maximum area? Which is most useful for finding the fixed perimeter?

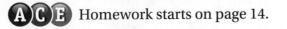 Homework starts on page 14.

Applications

1. Find the maximum area for a rectangle with a perimeter of 120 meters. Make your answer convincing by including these things:

   - Sketches of rectangles with a perimeter of 120 meters (Include rectangles that do not have the maximum area and the rectangle you think does have the maximum area.)

   - A table of lengths and areas for rectangles with a perimeter of 120 meters (Use increments of 5 meters for the lengths.)

   - A graph of the relationship between length and area

   Explain how each piece of evidence supports your answer.

2. What is the maximum area for a rectangle with a perimeter of 130 meters? As in Exercise 1, support your answer with sketches, a table, and a graph.

3. The graph shows the length and area of rectangles with a fixed perimeter. Use the graph for parts (a)–(e).

   a. Describe the shape of the graph and any special features.

   b. What is the maximum area for a rectangle with this fixed perimeter? What are the dimensions of this rectangle?

   c. Is there a rectangle with the least possible area? Explain.

   d. What is the area of a rectangle with a length of 3 centimeters?

   e. Describe two ways to find the fixed perimeter for the rectangles represented by the graph.

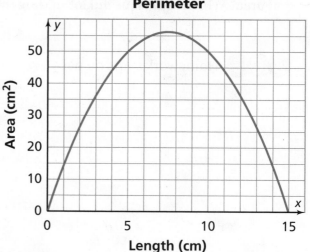

Rectangles With a Fixed Perimeter

4. Use the graph from Exercise 3. Make a table of values for the length and area.

   a. How is the shape of the graph reflected in the table?

   b. How can you use the table to find the maximum area and the dimensions of the rectangle with this area? Explain.

5. Hillsdale Farms wants to add a small, rectangular petting zoo for the public. They have a fixed amount of fencing to use for the zoo. This graph shows the lengths and areas of the rectangles they can make.

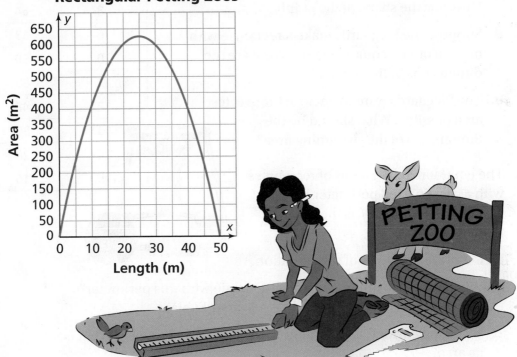

Rectangular Petting Zoos

   a. Describe the shape of the graph and any special features you observe.

   b. What is the greatest area possible for a rectangle with this perimeter? What are the dimensions of this rectangle?

   c. What is the area of the rectangle with a length of 10 meters? What is the area of the rectangle with a length of 40 meters? How are these rectangles related?

   d. What are the dimensions of the rectangle with an area of 600 square meters?

   e. What is the fixed amount of fencing available for the petting zoo? Explain.

6. The lifeguards at a beach want to place a rectangular boundary around the swimming area that can be used for water basketball. They have a fixed amount of rope to make the boundary. They use the table at the right to look at possible arrangements.

Rectangular Swimming Area

Length (m)	Area (m²)
1	15
2	28
3	39
4	48
5	55
6	60
7	63
8	64
9	63
10	60
11	55
12	48
13	39
14	28
15	15

  a. What patterns do you observe in the table?

  b. What is the fixed perimeter for the possible swimming areas?

  c. Sketch a graph of the data (*length, area*). Describe the shape of the graph.

  d. Suppose the lifeguards make a rectangle with an area of 11.5 square meters. What are the dimensions of the rectangle?

  e. The lifeguards want to enclose the greatest area possible. What should be the dimensions of the swimming area?

7. The equation for the areas of rectangles with a certain fixed perimeter is $A = \ell(20 - \ell)$, where ℓ is the length in meters.

  a. Describe the graph of this equation.

  b. What is the maximum area for a rectangle with this perimeter? What dimensions correspond to this area? Explain.

  c. A rectangle with this perimeter has a length of 15 meters. What is its area?

  d. Describe two ways you can find the perimeter. What is the perimeter?

8. A rectangle has a perimeter of 50 meters and a side length of ℓ.

   a. Express the other dimension of the rectangle in terms of ℓ.

   b. Write an equation for the area A in terms of ℓ.

   c. Sketch a graph of your equation and describe its shape.

   d. Use your equation to find the area of the rectangle with a length of 10 meters.

   e. How could you find the area in part (d) by using your graph?

   f. How could you find the area in part (d) by using a table?

   g. What is the maximum area possible for a rectangle with a perimeter of 50 meters? What are the dimensions of this rectangle?

9. A rectangle has a perimeter of 30 meters and a side length of ℓ.

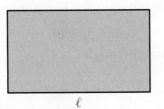

ℓ

   a. Express the other dimension of the rectangle in terms of ℓ.

   b. Write an equation for the area A in terms of ℓ.

   c. Make a graph of your equation and describe its shape.

   d. Use your equation to find the area of the rectangle with a length of 10 meters.

   e. How could you find the area in part (d) by using your graph?

   f. How could you find the area in part (d) by using a table?

   g. What is the maximum area possible for a rectangle with a perimeter of 30 meters? What are the dimensions of this rectangle?

10. **a.** Copy and complete the graph to show areas for rectangles with a fixed perimeter and lengths greater than 3 meters.

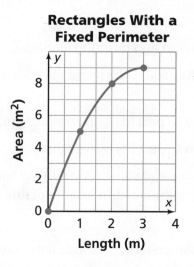

Rectangles With a Fixed Perimeter

Area (m²) vs Length (m)

b. Make a table of data for this situation.

c. What is the maximum area for a rectangle with this perimeter? What are the dimensions of this rectangle?

11. **Multiple Choice** Which equation describes the graph in Exercise 10?

A. $A = \ell(\ell - 6)$

B. $A = \ell(12 - \ell)$

C. $A = \ell(6 - \ell)$

D. $A = \ell(3 - \ell)$

12. **a.** Copy and complete the table to show areas for rectangles with a fixed perimeter and a length greater than 4 meters.

b. Make a graph of the relationship between length and area.

c. What are the dimensions of the rectangle with the maximum area?

13. **Multiple Choice** Which equation describes the data in the table in Exercise 12?

F. $A = \ell(8 - \ell)$

G. $A = \ell(16 - \ell)$

H. $A = \ell(4 - \ell)$

J. $A = \ell(\ell - 8)$

Rectangles With a Fixed Perimeter

Length (m)	Area (m²)
0	0
1	7
2	12
3	15
4	16
5	▪
6	▪
7	▪
8	▪

14. The equation $p = d(100 - d)$ gives the monthly profit p a photographer will earn if she charges d dollars for each print.

   a. Make a table and a graph for this equation.

   b. Estimate the price that will produce the maximum profit. Explain.

   c. How are the table and graph for this situation similar to those you made in Problem 1.1? How are they different?

Connections

15. Of all the rectangles with whole-number side lengths and an area of 20 square centimeters, which has the least perimeter? Explain.

16. **Multiple Choice** What does $2(-3 + 5) + 7 \times (-4) + (-1)$ equal?

   A. -55 **B.** -45 **C.** -31 **D.** -25

17. Eduardo's neighborhood association subdivided a large rectangular field into two playing fields as shown in the diagram.

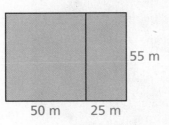

55 m

50 m   25 m

   a. Write expressions showing two ways you could calculate the area of the large field.

   b. Use the diagram and your expressions in part (a) to explain the Distributive Property.

For Exercises 18–21, use the Distributive Property to write the expression in expanded form. Then, simplify.

   18. $21(5 + 6)$ **19.** $2(35 + 1)$ **20.** $12(10 - 2)$ **21.** $9(3 + 5)$

For Exercises 22–24, use the Distributive Property to write the expression in factored form.

   22. $15 + 6$ **23.** $42 + 27$ **24.** $12 + 120$

For Exercises 25 and 26, solve each equation.

25. $5x - 30 = 95$ **26.** $22 + 4x = 152 - 9x$

For Exercises 27–30, do the following:

- Describe the pattern of change for each function.

- Describe how the pattern of change would look in a graph and in a table. Give as many details as you can without making a graph or table.

27. $y = 5x + 12$ **28.** $y = 10 - 3x$

29. $y = 3^x$ **30.** $y = \frac{15}{x}$

31. A rectangular soccer field has a perimeter of 400 yards. The equation $\ell = 200 - w$ represents the relationship between the length ℓ and width w of the field.

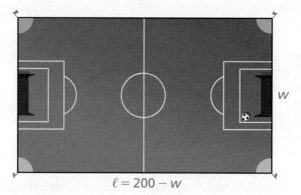

$\ell = 200 - w$

    a. Explain why the equation is correct.

    b. Is the relationship between length and width a quadratic function? Explain.

    c. Suppose a field is a nonrectangular parallelogram with a perimeter of 400 yards. Is the relationship between the side lengths the same as it is for the rectangular field?

    d. Suppose a field is a quadrilateral that is not a parallelogram. The perimeter of the field is 400 yards. Is the relationship between the side lengths the same as it is for the rectangular field?

32. Mr. DeAngelo is designing a school building. The music room floor will be a rectangle with an area of 1,200 square feet.

    a. Make a table showing a range of possible lengths and widths for the music room floor for ten different room arrangements.

    b. Add a column to your table for the perimeter of each rectangle.

    c. What patterns do you see in the perimeter column? What kinds of rectangles have large perimeters? What kinds have small perimeters?

    d. Write an equation you can use to calculate the length of the floor for any given width.

Extensions

33. A beach has a rectangular swimming area for toddlers. One side of the swimming area is the shore. Buoys and a rope with a length of 20 meters are used to form the other three sides.

    a. How should you arrange the rope to make a rectangle with the maximum area?

    b. In Problem 1.1, a fixed length of 20 meters is also used to form a rectangle. Compare the rectangle with maximum area in that Problem to the rectangle with maximum area in part (a). Are the shapes and areas of the rectangles the same? Explain.

    c. Make a graph relating the length and area for the possible rectangular swimming areas. How does the graph compare with the graph from Problem 1.1?

Mathematical Reflections

1

In this Investigation, you looked at the relationship between length and area for rectangles with a fixed perimeter. You learned that this relationship is a quadratic function. The following questions will help you summarize what you have learned.

Think about these questions. Discuss your ideas with other students and your teacher. Then write a summary of your findings in your notebook.

1. a. Describe the characteristics of graphs and tables of quadratic functions you have observed so far.

   b. How do the patterns in a graph of a quadratic function appear in the table of values for the function?

2. Describe two ways to find the maximum area for rectangles with a fixed perimeter.

3. How are tables, graphs, and equations for quadratic functions different from those for linear and exponential functions?

Common Core Mathematical Practices

As you worked on the Problems in this Investigation, you used prior knowledge to make sense of them. You also applied Mathematical Practices to solve the Problems. Think back over your work, the ways you thought about the Problems, and how you used Mathematical Practices.

Elena described her thoughts in the following way:

> We noticed that the relationship between length and area was not an exponential or linear function. As the length increased by 1, the area did not grow by a constant factor or constant amount. The graph did not look like that of a linear or exponential function.
>
> ....
>
> **Common Core Standards for Mathematical Practice**
>
> **MP7** Look for and make use of structure.

? • What other Mathematical Practices can you identify in Elena's reasoning?

• Describe a Mathematical Practice that you and your classmates used to solve a different Problem in this Investigation.

2

Quadratic Expressions

In the last Problem, you used the lengths of rectangles with a fixed perimeter to write an expression that represents their area. *Length* was the independent variable, and *area* was the dependent variable. In this Investigation, you will continue to write expressions using area as a context.

2.1 Trading Land
Representing Areas of Rectangles

Suppose you give a friend two $1 bills, and your friend gives you eight quarters.

- Would you consider this a fair trade?

Common Core State Standards

A-SSE.A.1 Interpret expressions that represent a quantity in terms of its context.

F-IF.B.4 For a function that models a relationship between two quantities, interpret key features of graphs and tables in terms of the quantities, and sketch graphs showing key features given a verbal description of the relationship.

F-IF.C.8 Write a function defined by an expression in different but equivalent forms to reveal and explain different properties of the function.

Also A-SSE.A.1a, A-SSE.A.1b, A-SSE.B.2, A-SSE.B.3, A-CED.A.2, A-REI.D.10, F-IF.C.7, F-IF.C.7a, F-IF.C.8a, F-BF.A.1, F-BF.A.1a

Sometimes it is not this easy to determine whether a trade is fair. Consider the following situation:

A developer has purchased all the land on a mall site except for one square lot. The lot measures 125 meters on each side. In exchange for the lot, the developer offers its owner a lot on another site. The plan for this lot is shown below.

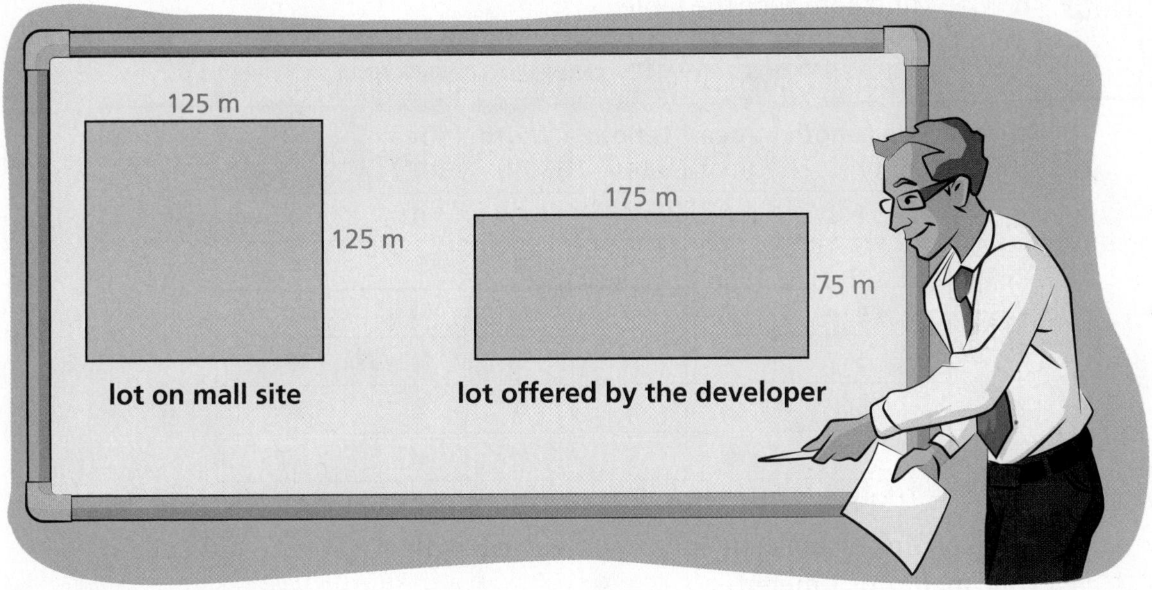

125 m

125 m

175 m

75 m

lot on mall site   lot offered by the developer

- Do you think this is a fair trade? Why or why not?

? How is the area of a square affected if one dimension is increased by *x* and the second dimension decreased by *x*? Explain.

In this Problem, you will look at a trade situation. See if you can find a pattern that will help you make predictions about more complex situations.

Problem 2.1

Suppose you trade a square lot for a rectangular lot. The length of the rectangular lot is 2 meters greater than the side length of the square lot, and the width is 2 meters less.

A **1.** Copy and complete the table.

Original Square		New Rectangle			Difference of Areas (m²)
Side Length (m)	Area (m²)	Length (m)	Width (m)	Area (m²)	
2	4	4	0	0	4
3	9	5	1	5	4
4	■	■	■	■	■
5	■	■	■	■	■
6	■	■	■	■	■
n	■	■	■	■	■

2. Explain why the table starts with a side length of 2 meters, rather than 0 meters or 1 meter.

3. For each side length, tell how the areas of the new and original lots compare. For which side lengths, if any, is the trade fair?

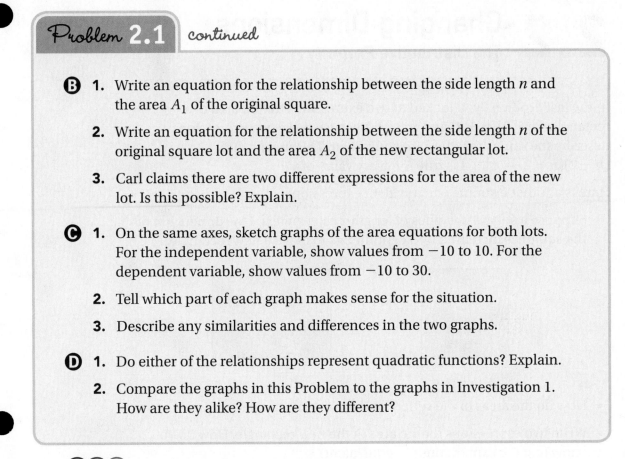

Problem **2.1** *continued*

B 1. Write an equation for the relationship between the side length n and the area A_1 of the original square.

2. Write an equation for the relationship between the side length n of the original square lot and the area A_2 of the new rectangular lot.

3. Carl claims there are two different expressions for the area of the new lot. Is this possible? Explain.

C 1. On the same axes, sketch graphs of the area equations for both lots. For the independent variable, show values from -10 to 10. For the dependent variable, show values from -10 to 30.

2. Tell which part of each graph makes sense for the situation.

3. Describe any similarities and differences in the two graphs.

D 1. Do either of the relationships represent quadratic functions? Explain.

2. Compare the graphs in this Problem to the graphs in Investigation 1. How are they alike? How are they different?

A C E Homework starts on page 38.

2.2 Changing Dimensions
The Distributive Property

In the last Problem, you looked at two expressions for the area of a rectangle: $(n - 2)(n + 2)$ and $n^2 - 4$. Because these two expressions describe the same area, they are equivalent. This means that $(n - 2)(n + 2) = n^2 - 4$ is true for every value of n.

Here is another example of equivalent expressions:

Suppose a square has sides of length x centimeters. One dimension of the square is increased by 3 centimeters to make a new rectangle.

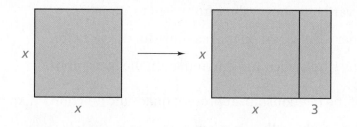

- How do the areas of the square and the new rectangle compare?

- Write two expressions for the area of the new rectangle. How do you know that the expressions are equivalent?

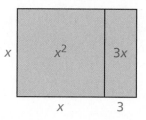

The expressions $x(x + 3)$ and $x^2 + 3x$ are examples of **quadratic expressions.** An expression in **factored form** is quadratic if it has exactly two *linear factors*, each with the variable raised to the first power. An expression in **expanded form** is quadratic if the highest power of the variable is 2. The expression $x(x + 3)$ is in factored form. The expression $x^2 + 3x$ is in expanded form.

The equation $x(x + 3) = x^2 + 3x$ is an example of the **Distributive Property,** which you studied in earlier Units. The Distributive Property says that, for any three numbers a, b, and c, $a(b + c) = ab + ac$.

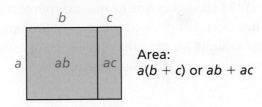

Area:
$a(b + c)$ or $ab + ac$

When you write $a(b + c)$ as $ab + ac$, you are multiplying, or writing the expression in expanded form. When you write $ab + ac$ as $a(b + c)$, you are factoring, or writing the expression in factored form.

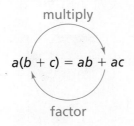

multiply

$a(b + c) = ab + ac$

factor

- Can you use the Distributive Property to show that $(n - 2)(n + 2) = n^2 - 4$?

The **terms** $2x$ and $3x$ are **like terms.** You can use the Distributive Property to add like terms. For example, $2x + 3x = (2 + 3)x = 5x$.

In this Problem, you will explore what happens to the area of a square when one or both of its dimensions change. You can use the Distributive Property to write equivalent expressions for area in both factored form and expanded form.

Problem 2.2

A Each rectangle is the result of changing one or more dimensions of a square. Each rectangle has been subdivided into two or four smaller rectangles. Write two expressions for the area of the rectangle outlined in red, one in factored form and one in expanded form.

1.

x · · · x · · · 6

2.

x · · · 6 · · · x

3. 2 · x · · · x · 5

4. 3 · x · · · x · 3

5. 2 · x · · · x · 4

6. 1 · x · · · x · x

B Use a rectangle model to write each expression in expanded form.

1. $(x + 3)(x + 5)$

2. $(4 + x)(4 + x)$

3. $3x(x + 1)$

Problem **2.2** *continued*

C Carminda says she does not need a rectangle model to multiply $(x + 3)$ by $(x + 5)$. She uses the Distributive Property.

$$
\begin{aligned}
(x+3)(x+5) &= (x+3)x + (x+3)5 &\quad (1)\\
&= x^2 + 3x + 5x + 15 &\quad (2)\\
&= x^2 + 8x + 15 &\quad (3)
\end{aligned}
$$

1. Is Carminda correct? Explain what she did at each step.

2. Show how using the Distributive Property to multiply $(x + 3)$ and $(x + 5)$ is the same as using a rectangle model.

D Use the Distributive Property to write each expression in expanded form.

1. $(x + 5)(x + 5)$

2. $(x - 4)(x + 3)$

3. $2x(5 - x)$

4. $(2x + 1)(5 - x)$

5. $(n - 2)(n + 2)$

E Write each expression in expanded form.

1. $(x + 7)^2$

2. $(x - 7)^2$

3. $(2n - 5)^2$

4. $(2n + 5)^2$

5. After doing similar problems like these, Lydia claims that she sees a pattern that would help her expand expressions in less time. What pattern do you think she observes?

A C E Homework starts on page 38.

2.3 Factoring Quadratic Expressions

Ms. Porath's class summarizes two ways to rewrite a factored expression, such as $(x + 2)(x + 6)$, in expanded form.

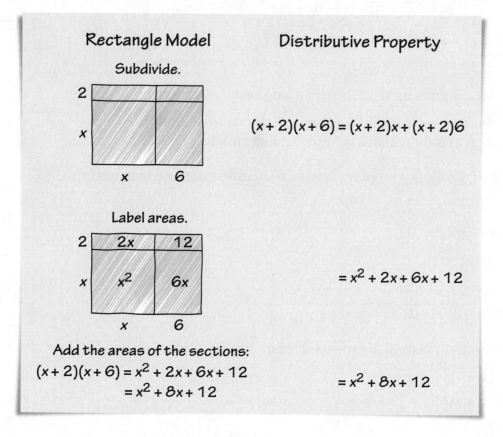

Rectangle Model

Subdivide.

Label areas.

Add the areas of the sections:
$(x + 2)(x + 6) = x^2 + 2x + 6x + 12$
$= x^2 + 8x + 12$

Distributive Property

$(x + 2)(x + 6) = (x + 2)x + (x + 2)6$

$= x^2 + 2x + 6x + 12$

$= x^2 + 8x + 12$

- How do these methods compare to the ones you and your classmates used?

In Problem 2.2, Question E, you expanded expressions like $(x + 3)^2$. The expression $(x + 3)^2$ is an example of a binomial squared. A **binomial** is an algebraic expression that is the sum or difference of two terms. For example, $x + 3$, $x - 4$, and $2x + 4$ are binomials. The two factors of a quadratic expression in factored form are examples of binomials. For example, in the factored form $(x + 2)(x + 6)$, $x + 2$ and $x + 6$ are binomials.

Lydia noticed the following pattern.

When you square a binomial, the expanded form has 3 terms.

$$(x + 3)^2 = x^2 + 6x + 9$$

- The first term is the square of the first term of the binomial: $x \cdot x$ or x^2

- The second term is twice the product of the two terms in the binomial: $2(x \cdot 3)$ or $6x$

- The third term is the square of the second term in the binomial: 3^2 or 9

- Is she correct? Explain.
- Is $x^2 + 8x + 12$ the square of a binomial? Explain.

You have used the Distributive Property to write quadratic expressions in expanded form. In the next Problem, you will use the Distributive Property to write expressions in factored form.

- How can you write an expanded expression, such as $x^2 + 8x + 12$, in factored form?

Problem **2.3**

A 1. Copy the diagram below. Replace each question mark with the correct length or area.

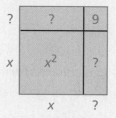

2. Write two expressions for the area of the rectangle outlined in red.

B Consider the expression $x^2 + bx + 8$.

1. Choose a value for b that gives an expression you can factor. Then, write the expression in factored form.

2. Compare your work with your classmates. Did everyone write the same expressions? Explain.

C For parts (1)–(3), find values of r and s that make the equations true.

1. $x^2 + 10x + 24 = (x + 6)(x + r)$

2. $x^2 + 11x + 24 = (x + s)(x + r)$

3. $x^2 + 25x + 24 = (x + r)(x + s)$

4. Describe the strategies you used to find the values of r and s in parts (1)–(3).

D Alyse sees a pattern in Question C. She says she can use the Distributive Property to factor the expression $x^2 + 10x + 16$. She writes:

$$x^2 + 10x + 16 = x^2 + 2x + 8x + 16 \qquad (1)$$
$$= x(x + 2) + 8(x + 2) \qquad (2)$$
$$= (x + 2)(x + 8) \qquad (3)$$

Is Alyse correct? Explain what she did at each step.

Problem **2.3** *continued*

E Use the Distributive Property to factor each expression.

1. $x^2 + 5x + 2x + 10$

2. $x^2 + 11x + 10$

3. $x^2 + 3x - 10$

4. $x^2 - 8x + 15$

5. $15 - 14x - x^2$

6. $2x^2 + 7x + 5$

F Recall the expressions for the area of the rectangle in Problem 2.1: $n^2 - 4$ and $(n - 2)(n + 2)$. The expression $n^2 - 4$ is a **difference of squares.** After factoring and expanding quadratic expressions, the students in Mr. Towle's class claimed they could use the Distributive Property to show that the expressions for the area of the rectangle in Problem 2.1 were equivalent.

1. Are the students correct? Can you use the Distributive Property to show that $n^2 - 4 = (n - 2)(n + 2)$? Explain.

2. What are the factors of each expression?

a. $x^2 - 9$

b. $x^2 - 25$

A C E Homework starts on page 38.

2.4 Quadratic Functions and Their Graphs

In Investigation 1, you saw that graphs of equations of the form $y = x(a - x)$ are parabolas. You know that the graph of this equation is a parabola. You also know that the expressions $x(a - x)$ and $ax - x^2$ are equivalent expressions.

The **x-intercepts** of the graph below are $(0, 0)$ and $(a, 0)$. The **y-intercept** is $(0, 0)$. The graph has a *maximum point*. The y-coordinate of the maximum point is the **maximum value** of the function.

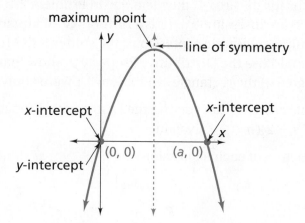

Some graphs, such as the graph of $y = -4 + x^2$, have a *minimum point*. The y-coordinate of the minimum point is the **minimum value** of the function.

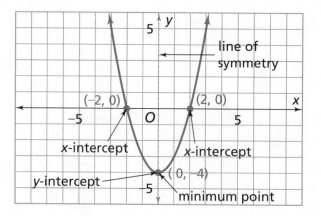

Milaka noticed that if you draw a vertical line from the minimum or maximum point to the *x*-axis and fold the graph along this line, the two halves of the parabola would match exactly. Her teacher said this line is called the **line of symmetry.**

- Does the line of symmetry divide the parabola into two identical parts? Explain.

In this Problem, you will explore the graphs of quadratic equations.

Problem 2.4

A The equations of several quadratic functions are given. For each function:

- Write an equivalent expression for *y* in expanded or factored form.
- Sketch a graph of the equation.
- Label the coordinates of the *x*- and *y*-intercepts.
- Label the maximum or minimum point.
- Draw the line of symmetry on your graph.

1. $y = x(x - 6)$ **2.** $y = 16 - x^2$

3. $y = x^2 + 6x + 9$ **4.** $y = x^2 + 9x + 20$

5. $y = x^2 + 5x - 14$ **6.** $y = (3 - x)(2 + x)$

B Without graphing, describe the graph of each equation. Give as many details as possible.

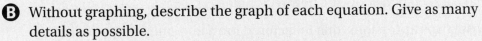

1. $y = x^2 + 8x + 12$ **2.** $y = (x + 3)(x - 3)$ **3.** $y = -x^2 + 6x$

4. Explain what features of the graph of a function, such as intercepts, maximum/minimum point, and line of symmetry, you can predict from an equation of the function. Describe how you can make these predictions.

A C E Homework starts on page 38.

Applications

1. A square has sides of length x centimeters. One dimension increases by 4 centimeters and the other decreases by 4 centimeters, forming a new rectangle.

   a. Make a table showing the side length and area of the square and the area of the new rectangle. Include whole-number x-values from 4 to 16.

   b. On the same axes, graph the data $(x, area)$ for both the square and the rectangle.

   c. Suppose you want to compare the area of a square with the area of the corresponding new rectangle. Is it easier to use the table or the graph?

   d. Write equations for the area of the original square and the area of the new rectangle in terms of x.

   e. Use your calculator to graph both equations. Show values of x from -10 to 10. Copy the graphs onto your paper. Describe the relationship between the two graphs.

2. A square has sides of length x centimeters. One dimension increases by 5 centimeters, forming a new rectangle.

   a. Make a sketch to show the new rectangle.

   b. Write two expressions, one in factored form and one in expanded form, for the area of the new rectangle.

   c. Choose one of your expressions from part (b). Use it to write an equation for the area A of the new rectangle in terms of x. Then, graph the equation.

For Exercises 3 and 4, draw a divided rectangle whose area is represented by each expression. Label the lengths and area of each section. Then, write an equivalent expression in expanded form.

3. $x(x + 7)$

4. $x(x - 3)$

For Exercises 5–7, draw a divided rectangle whose area is represented by each expression. Label the lengths and area of each section. Then, write an equivalent expression in factored form.

5. $x^2 + 6x$ **6.** $x^2 - 8x$ **7.** $x^2 - x$

For Exercises 8–11, write the expression in factored form.

8. $x^2 + 10x$ **9.** $x^2 - 6x$ **10.** $x^2 + 11x$ **11.** $x^2 - 2x$

For Exercises 12–15, write the expression in expanded form.

12. $x(x + 1)$ **13.** $x(x - 10)$ **14.** $x(x + 6)$ **15.** $x(x - 15)$

For Exercises 16–20, write two expressions, one in factored form and one in expanded form, for the area of the rectangle outlined in red.

16.   **17.**   **18.**

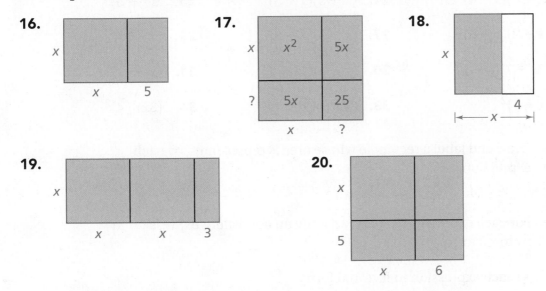

19.   **20.**

21. A square has sides of length x meters. Both dimensions increase by 5 meters, forming a new square.

   a. Make a sketch to show the new square.

   b. Write two expressions, one in factored form and one in expanded form, for the area of the new square.

   c. Choose one of your expressions from part (b). Use it to write an equation for the area A of the new square in terms of x. Then, graph the equation. Does the equation represent a quadratic function? Explain.

22. A square has sides of length x centimeters. One dimension increases by 4 centimeters and the other increases by 5 centimeters, forming a new rectangle.

   a. Make a sketch to show the new rectangle.

   b. Write two expressions, one in factored form and one in expanded form, for the area of the new rectangle.

   c. Choose one of your expressions from part (b). Use it to write an equation for the area A of the new square in terms of x. Then, graph the equation. Does the equation represent a quadratic function? Explain.

For Exercises 23–34, use the Distributive Property to write each expression in expanded form.

23. $(x - 3)(x + 4)$ **24.** $(x + 3)(x + 5)$ **25.** $x(x + 5)$

26. $(x - 2)(x - 6)$ **27.** $(x - 3)(x + 3)$ **28.** $(x - 3)(x + 5)$

29. $(2x + 1)(x + 1)$ **30.** $(x - 1)(7x + 1)$ **31.** $(x - 1)(3x - 3)$

32. $(x + 7)^2$ **33.** $(3x + 4)^2$ **34.** $(3x - 4)^2$

35. **a.** Draw and label a rectangle whose area is represented by each expression.

$$x^2 + 3x + 4x + 12 \qquad x^2 + 7x + 10$$

   b. For each expression in part (a), write an equivalent expression in factored form.

36. Write each expression in factored form.

   a. $x^2 + 13x + 12$ **b.** $x^2 - 13x + 12$ **c.** $x^2 + 8x + 12$

   d. $x^2 - 8x + 12$ **e.** $x^2 + 7x + 12$ **f.** $x^2 - 7x + 12$

   g. $x^2 + 11x - 12$ **h.** $x^2 - 11x - 12$ **i.** $x^2 + 4x - 12$

   j. $x^2 - 4x - 12$ **k.** $x^2 + x - 12$ **l.** $x^2 - x - 12$

37. Write each expression in expanded form. Look for a pattern. Make a generalization about the expanded form of expressions of the form $(x + a)(x + a)$.

  a. $(x + 1)(x + 1)$ **b.** $(x + 5)(x + 5)$ **c.** $(x - 5)(x - 5)$

38. Write each expression in expanded form. Look for a pattern. Make a generalization about the expanded form of expressions of the form $(x + a)(x - a)$.

  a. $(x + 1)(x - 1)$ **b.** $(x + 5)(x - 5)$ **c.** $(x + 1.5)(x - 1.5)$

39. Use your generalizations from Exercises 37 and 38 to write each of these expressions in factored form.

  a. $x^2 + 6x + 9$ **b.** $x^2 - 6x + 9$

  c. $x^2 - 9$ **d.** $x^2 - 16$

40. Write each expression in factored form.

  a. $2x^2 + 5x + 3$ **b.** $4x^2 - 9$ **c.** $4x^2 + 12x + 9$

41. Write each difference of squares in factored form.

  a. $x^2 - 49$ **b.** $4x^2 - 49$ **c.** $25x^2 - 1.44$

For Exercises 42–50, determine whether the equation represents a quadratic function *without* making a table or a graph. Explain.

42. $y = 5x + x^2$ **43.** $y = 2x + 8$ **44.** $y = (9 - x)x$

45. $y = 4x(3 + x)$ **46.** $y = 3^x$ **47.** $y = x^2 + 10x$

48. $y = x(x + 4)$ **49.** $y = 2(x + 4)$ **50.** $y = 7x + 10 + x^2$

51. Rewrite each equation in expanded form. Then, give the x- and y-intercepts, the coordinates of the maximum or minimum point, and the line of symmetry for the graph of each equation.

  a. $y = (x - 3)(x + 3)$ **b.** $y = x(x + 5)$ **c.** $y = (x + 3)(x + 5)$

  d. $y = (x - 3)(x + 5)$ **e.** $y = (x + 3)(x - 5)$ **f.** $y = x(x - 3)$

For Exercises 52 and 53, complete parts (a)–(e).

    a. Find an equivalent factored form of the equation.

    b. Identify the x- and y-intercepts for the graph of the equation.

    c. Find the coordinates of the maximum or minimum point.

    d. Find the line of symmetry.

    e. Tell which form of the equation can be used to predict the features in parts (b)–(d) without making a graph.

52. $y = x^2 + 5x + 6$ **53.** $y = x^2 - 25$

54. Darnell makes a rectangle from a square by doubling one dimension and adding 3 centimeters. He leaves the other dimension unchanged.

    a. Write an equation for the area A of the new rectangle in terms of the side length x of the original square.

    b. Graph your area equation.

    c. What are the x-intercepts of the graph? How can you find the x-intercepts from the graph? How can you find them from the equation?

Connections

55. The winner of the Jammin' Jelly jingle contest will receive $500. Antonia and her friends are writing a jingle. They plan to divide the prize money equally if they win.

    a. Suppose n friends write the winning jingle. How much prize money will each person receive?

    b. Describe the relationship between the number of friends and the prize money each friend receives.

    c. Write a question about this relationship that is easier to answer by making a graph. Write a question that is easier to answer by making a table. Write a question that is easier to answer by writing an equation.

    d. Is this relationship a quadratic function, a linear function, an exponential function, or an inverse variation? Explain.

56. The Stellar International Cellular long-distance company and the
Call Any Time company have different charge plans.

No monthly
service fee

$.95 per min
Call Any Time Co.

$13.95/mo
$.39/min

Stellar
International
Cellular

    a. Represent each charge plan with an equation, a table, and
a graph.

    b. For each plan, tell whether the relationship between calling
time and monthly cost is a quadratic function, a linear function,
an exponential function, or an inverse variation. How do your
equation, table, and graph support your answer?

    c. For what number of minutes are the costs for the two plans equal?

57. A square has sides of length x centimeters.

    a. The square is enlarged by a scale factor of 2. What is the area of
the enlarged square?

    b. How does the area of the original square compare with the area of
the enlarged square?

    c. Is the new square similar to the original square? Explain.

58. A rectangle has dimensions of x centimeters and $(x + 1)$ centimeters.

    a. The rectangle is enlarged by a scale factor of 2. What is the area of
the enlarged rectangle?

    b. How does the area of the original rectangle compare with the area
of the enlarged rectangle?

    c. Is the new rectangle similar to the original rectangle? Explain.

59. Suppose the circumference of a cross section of a tree is *x* feet.

a. What is the diameter in terms of *x*?

b. What is the radius in terms of *x*?

c. What is the area of the cross section in terms of *x*?

d. Is the relationship between the circumference and the area of the cross section linear, quadratic, exponential, or none of these?

e. Suppose the circumference of the cross section is 10 feet. What are the diameter, radius, and area of the cross section?

60. For each polygon, write formulas for the perimeter *P* and area *A* in terms of ℓ if it is possible. If it is not possible to write a formula, explain why.

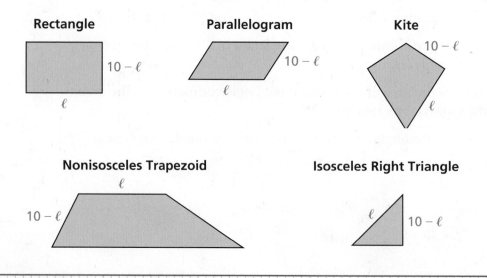

Rectangle

$10 - \ell$

ℓ

Parallelogram

$10 - \ell$

ℓ

Kite

$10 - \ell$

ℓ

Nonisosceles Trapezoid

ℓ

$10 - \ell$

Isosceles Right Triangle

ℓ

$10 - \ell$

61. a. Write the equation of the line that passes through the two points shown.

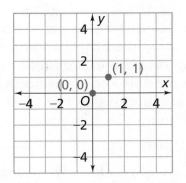

b. Is there a different line that can be drawn through these points? Explain.

For Exercises 62–65, evaluate the expression for the given values of x.

62. $x(x - 5)$ for $x = 2$ and $x = 3$

63. $3x^2 - x$ for $x = 1$ and $x = \frac{1}{3}$

64. $x^2 + 5x + 4$ for $x = 2$ and $x = -4$

65. $(x - 7)(x + 2)$ for $x = -2$ and $x = 2$

Extensions

66. Multiple Choice Which expression is equivalent to $(2n + 3)(4n + 2)$?

A. $8n + 5$

B. $6n^2 + 7n + 4n + 5$

C. $8n^2 + 16n + 6$

D. $8n^2 + 6$

For Exercises 67 and 68, write each expression in factored form. You may want to draw a rectangle model.

67. $2x^2 + 3x + 1$

68. $4x^2 + 10x + 6$

69. Sketch graphs of the equations $y = x^2 + 2x$ and $y = x^2 + 2$.

a. How are the graphs similar?

b. How are the graphs different?

c. Find the y-intercept for each graph.

d. Find the x-intercepts for each graph if they exist. If there are no x-intercepts, explain why.

e. Do all quadratic functions have y-intercepts? Explain.

In this Investigation, you wrote quadratic expressions to represent areas of rectangles formed by changing the dimensions of a square. You rewrote expressions in different forms by using rectangular models and by using the Distributive Property. You looked at the equations and graphs of functions. The following questions will help you summarize what you have learned.

Think about these questions. Discuss your ideas with other students and your teacher. Then write a summary of your findings in your notebook.

1. Explain **how** you can use the Distributive Property to answer each question. Use examples to help with your explanations.

   a. Suppose a quadratic expression is in factored form. **How** can you find an equivalent expression in expanded form?

   b. Suppose a quadratic expression is in expanded form. **How** can you find an equivalent expression in factored form?

2. **Describe** what you know about the shape of the graph of a quadratic function. Include important features of the graph and describe how you can predict these features from the equation of the function.

Common Core Mathematical Practices

As you worked on the Problems in this Investigation, you used prior knowledge to make sense of them. You also applied Mathematical Practices to solve the Problems. Think back over your work, the ways you thought about the Problems, and how you used Mathematical Practices.

Hector described his thoughts in the following way:

We thought it was interesting how you can use equivalent expressions to represent the area of a rectangle in Problems 2.2 and 2.3. Le Von reminded us that the area model also represented the Distributive Property. In our group, we used the Distributive Property to factor or expand quadratic expressions. But we still thought that the area model might be helpful to factor more complex quadratic expressions.

Common Core Standards for Mathematical Practice

MP8 Look for and express regularity in repeated reasoning.

? • What other Mathematical Practices can you identify in Hector's reasoning?

• Describe a Mathematical Practice that you and your classmates used to solve a different Problem in this Investigation.

Quadratic Patterns of Change

In previous Units, you studied patterns in linear and exponential functions. In this Investigation, you will look for patterns in quadratic functions as you solve some interesting counting problems.

- What patterns of change characterize linear and exponential functions?

- What patterns of change did you notice in the quadratic functions in Investigations 1 and 2?

3.1 Exploring Triangular Numbers

Study the pattern of dots.

Figure 1   Figure 2   Figure 3   Figure 4

The numbers that represent the number of dots in each triangle are called **triangular numbers.** The first triangular number is 1, the second triangular number is 3, the third is 6, the fourth is 10, and so on.

> ? How many dots do you predict will be in Figure 5? In Figure n?

Common Core State Standards

A-SSE.A.2 Use the structure of an expression to identify ways to rewrite it.

F-IF.C.7 Graph functions expressed symbolically and show key features of the graph . . .

F-BF.A.1 Write a function that describes a relationship between two quantities.

Also A-SSE.A.1b, A-CED.A.2, A-REI.D.10, F-IF.B.4, F-IF.C.7a, F-IF.C.9, F-BF.A.1a, F-LE.A.1

Problem 3.1

You can also represent triangular numbers with patterns of squares.
The number of squares in Figure n is the nth triangular number.

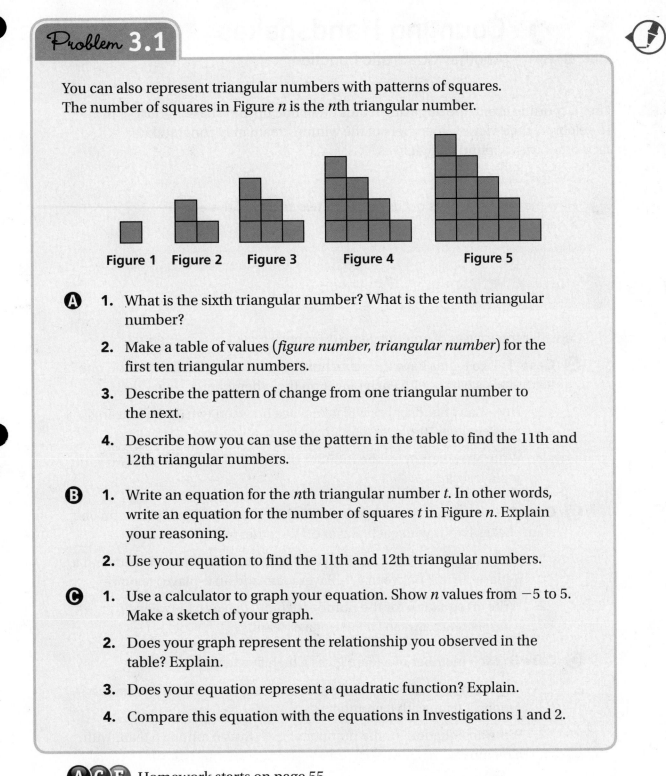

Figure 1   Figure 2   Figure 3   Figure 4   Figure 5

A **1.** What is the sixth triangular number? What is the tenth triangular number?

    2. Make a table of values (*figure number, triangular number*) for the first ten triangular numbers.

    3. Describe the pattern of change from one triangular number to the next.

    4. Describe how you can use the pattern in the table to find the 11th and 12th triangular numbers.

B **1.** Write an equation for the nth triangular number t. In other words, write an equation for the number of squares t in Figure n. Explain your reasoning.

    2. Use your equation to find the 11th and 12th triangular numbers.

C **1.** Use a calculator to graph your equation. Show n values from -5 to 5. Make a sketch of your graph.

    2. Does your graph represent the relationship you observed in the table? Explain.

    3. Does your equation represent a quadratic function? Explain.

    4. Compare this equation with the equations in Investigations 1 and 2.

A C E Homework starts on page 55.

3.2 Counting Handshakes
Another Quadratic Function

After a sporting event, the opposing teams often line up and shake hands. To celebrate their victory, members of the winning team may congratulate each other with a round of high fives.

> (?) How many handshakes occur between two teams at the end of a game?

Problem 3.2

Consider three cases of greeting team members:

A **Case 1** Two teams have the same number of players. Each player on one team shakes hands with each player on the other team.

1. How many handshakes will take place between two 5-player teams? Between two 10-player teams?

2. Write an equation for the number of handshakes h between two n-player teams.

B **Case 2** One team has one fewer player than the other. Each player on one team shakes hands with each player on the other team.

1. How many handshakes will take place between a 7-player team and a 6-player team? Between a 9-player team and an 8-player team?

2. Write an equation for the number of handshakes h between an n-player team and an $(n - 1)$-player team.

C **Case 3** Each member of a team gives a high five to each teammate.

1. How many high fives will take place among a team with 4 members? Among a team with 8 members?

2. Write an equation for the number of high fives h among a team with n members.

D Compare the three equations from Questions A–C. Do they represent quadratic functions? Explain.

A C E Homework starts on page 55.

3.3 Examining Patterns of Change

In this Problem, you will examine the patterns of change that characterize quadratic relationships.

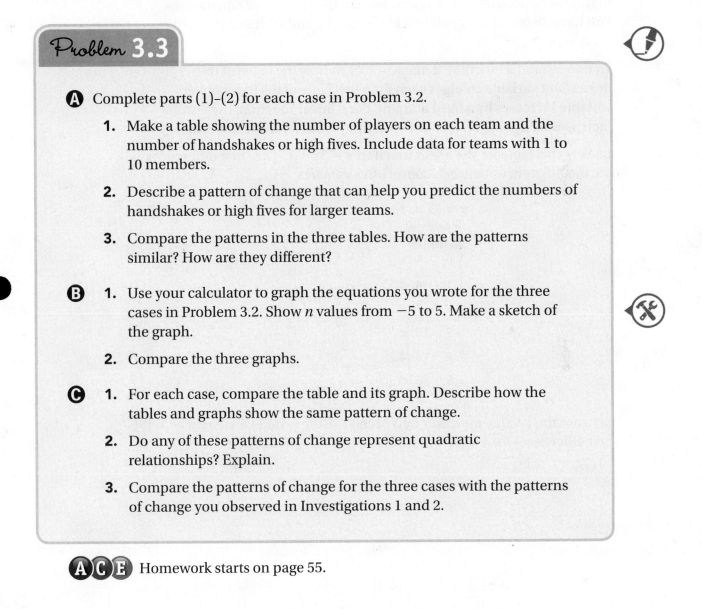

Problem 3.3

Ⓐ Complete parts (1)–(2) for each case in Problem 3.2.

1. Make a table showing the number of players on each team and the number of handshakes or high fives. Include data for teams with 1 to 10 members.

2. Describe a pattern of change that can help you predict the numbers of handshakes or high fives for larger teams.

3. Compare the patterns in the three tables. How are the patterns similar? How are they different?

Ⓑ 1. Use your calculator to graph the equations you wrote for the three cases in Problem 3.2. Show *n* values from −5 to 5. Make a sketch of the graph.

2. Compare the three graphs.

Ⓒ 1. For each case, compare the table and its graph. Describe how the tables and graphs show the same pattern of change.

2. Do any of these patterns of change represent quadratic relationships? Explain.

3. Compare the patterns of change for the three cases with the patterns of change you observed in Investigations 1 and 2.

ⒶⒸⒺ Homework starts on page 55.

3.4 Quadratic Functions and Patterns of Change

You have used equations to model a variety of quadratic functions. You may have noticed some common characteristics of these equations. You have also observed patterns in the graphs and tables of quadratic functions.

To understand a function, it helps to look at how the value of the dependent variable changes each time the value of the independent variable increases by a fixed amount. For a linear function, the y-value increases by a constant amount each time the x-value increases by 1.

Look at this table for the linear function $y = 3x + 1$. The "first differences" are the differences between consecutive y-values.

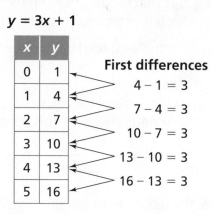

$y = 3x + 1$

x	y
0	1
1	4
2	7
3	10
4	13
5	16

First differences

$4 - 1 = 3$

$7 - 4 = 3$

$10 - 7 = 3$

$13 - 10 = 3$

$16 - 13 = 3$

Because the y-value increases by 3 each time the x-value increases by 1, the first differences for $y = 3x + 1$ are all a constant amount of 3.

The simplest quadratic function is $y = x^2$, and it is the rule for generating square numbers. In fact, the word *quadratic* comes from the Latin word for "square," *quadratus*.

The table shows that the first differences for $y = x^2$ are not constant.

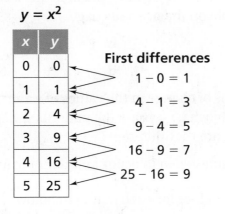

- What is the pattern of change for $y = x^2$?

Study the pattern of first and second differences for $y = x^2$.

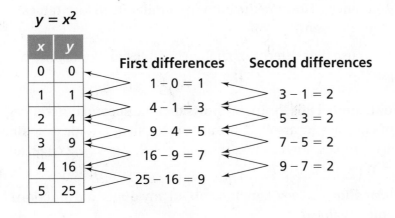

> ? Will the tables for other quadratic functions show a similar pattern? Explain.

Problem 3.4

Ⓐ 1. Make a table of values for each quadratic equation below. Include integer values of x from -5 to 5. Show the first and second differences as is done for the table on the previous page.

    a. $y = 2x(x + 3)$ **b.** $y = 3x - x^2$

    c. $y = (x - 2)^2$ **d.** $y = x^2 + 5x + 6$

    2. Consider the patterns of change in the values of y and in the first and second differences. In what ways are the patterns similar for the four tables? In what ways are they different?

    3. What patterns of change seem to occur for quadratic functions?

Ⓑ 1. Make a table of (x, y) values for each equation below. Show the first and second differences.

    a. $y = x + 2$ **b.** $y = 2x$ **c.** $y = 2^x$ **d.** $y = x^2$

    2. Consider the patterns of change in the values of y and in the first and second differences. How are the patterns similar in all four tables? How are they different?

    3. How can you use the patterns of change in tables to identify the type of function?

Ⓒ 1. The introduction of this Problem shows that the second differences for the function $y = x^2$ are all 2. Is this true for all quadratic functions? Try some examples, such as $y = 2x^2$, $y = x^2 + 2$, $y = x^2 + 2x + 2$, and $y = 3x^2 + x$.

    2. What information can you conclude about any quadratic function from a table of values?

Ⓐ Ⓒ Ⓔ Homework starts on page 55.

Applications

1. These dot patterns represent the first four *square numbers,* 1, 4, 9, and 16.

| Figure 1 | Figure 2 | Figure 3 | Figure 4 |

a. What are the next two square numbers?

b. Write an equation for the *n*th square number *s.*

c. Make a table and a graph of (*n, s*) values for the first ten square numbers. Describe the pattern of change from one square number to the next.

2. The numbers of dots in the figures below are the first four *rectangular numbers.*

| Figure 1 | Figure 2 | Figure 3 | Figure 4 |

a. What are the first four rectangular numbers?

b. Find the next two rectangular numbers.

c. Describe the pattern of change from one rectangular number to the next.

d. Predict the seventh and eighth rectangular numbers.

e. Write an equation for the *n*th rectangular number *r.*

3. In Problem 3.1, you looked at triangular numbers.

    a. What is the 18th triangular number?

    b. Is 210 a triangular number? Explain.

Did You Know?

Carl Friedrich Gauss (1777–1855) was a German mathematician and astronomer. When Gauss was about eight years old, his teacher asked his class to find the sum of the first 100 counting numbers. Gauss had the answer almost immediately!

Gauss realized that he could pair up the numbers as shown. Each pair has a sum of 101.

$$101$$
$$101$$
$$101$$
$$1 + 2 + 3 + 4 + 5 + \ldots + 96 + 97 + 98 + 99 + 100$$
$$101$$
$$101$$
$$101$$

There are 100 numbers, so there are 50 pairs. This means the sum is

$50 \times 101 = 5{,}050 \left[\text{or } \frac{100}{2}(101) \text{ or } \frac{100}{2} \text{ (first number plus last number)} \right].$

---

4. a. In Problem 3.1, you found an equation for the nth triangular number. Sam claims he can use this equation to find the sum of the first ten counting numbers. Explain why Sam is correct.

    b. What is the sum of the first ten counting numbers?

    c. What is the sum of the first 15 counting numbers?

    d. What is the sum of the first n counting numbers?

For Exercises 5–8, tell whether the number is a triangular number, a square number, a rectangular number, or none of these. Explain.

5. 110   **6.** 66   **7.** 121   **8.** 60

9. In a middle school math league, each team has six student members and two coaches.

  a. At the start of a match, the coaches and student members of one team exchange handshakes with the coaches and student members of the other team. How many handshakes occur?

  b. At the end of the match, the members and coaches of the winning team exchange high fives. How many high fives occur?

  c. The members of one team exchange handshakes with their coaches. How many handshakes occur?

10. In a 100-meter race, five runners are from the United States and three runners are from Canada.

  a. How many handshakes occur if the runners from one country exchange handshakes with the runners from the other country?

  b. How many high fives occur if the runners from the United States exchange high fives?

11. A company rents five offices in a building. There is a cable connecting each pair of offices.

  a. How many cables are there in all?

  b. Suppose the company rents two more offices. How many cables will they need in all?

  c. Compare this situation with Case 3 in Problem 3.2.

For Exercises 12–15, describe a situation that can be represented by the equation. Tell what the variables p and n represent in that situation.

12. $p = n(n - 1)$ **13.** $p = 2n$

14. $p = n(n - 2)$ **15.** $p = n(16 - n)$

16. The graphs below represent situations you have looked at in this Unit.

Graph I

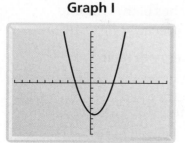

Graph II

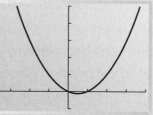

Graph III

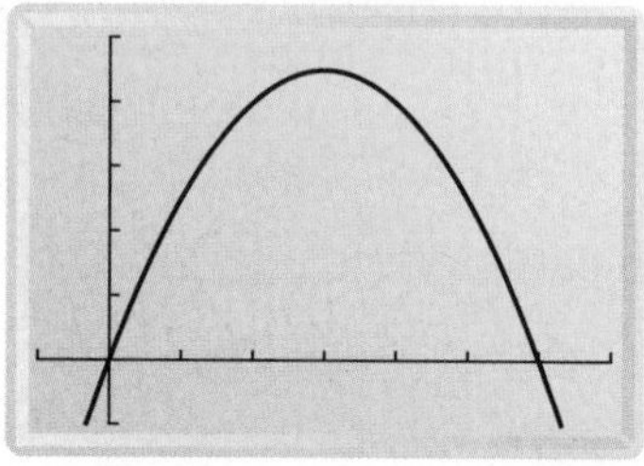

Graph IV

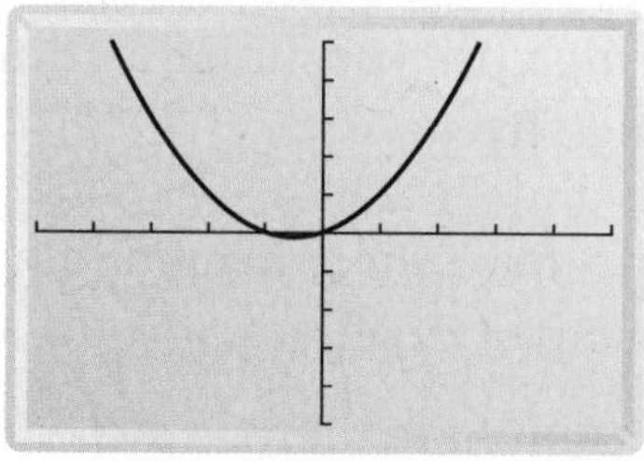

a. Which graph might represent the number of high fives exchanged among a team with n players? Explain.

b. Which graph might represent the areas of rectangles with a fixed perimeter?

c. Which graph might represent the areas of a rectangle formed by increasing one dimension of a square by 2 centimeters and decreasing the other dimension by 3 centimeters?

d. Which graph might represent a triangular-number pattern?

For Exercises 17–19, the tables represent quadratic functions. Copy and complete each table.

17.

x	y
0	0
1	1
2	3
3	6
4	■
5	■
6	■

18.

x	y
0	0
1	3
2	8
3	15
4	■
5	■
6	■

19.

x	y
0	0
1	4
2	6
3	6
4	■
5	■
6	■

For Exercises 20–24, tell whether the table represents a quadratic function. If it does, tell whether the function has a maximum or minimum value.

20.

x	−3	−2	−1	0	1	2	3	4	5
y	−4	1	4	5	4	1	−4	−11	−18

21.

x	0	1	2	3	4	5	6	7	8
y	2	3	6	11	18	27	38	51	66

22.

x	0	1	2	3	4	5	6	7	8
y	0	−4	−6	−6	−4	0	6	14	24

23.

x	−4	−3	−2	−1	0	1	2	3	4
y	5	4	3	2	1	2	3	4	5

24.

x	−4	−3	−2	−1	0	1	2	3	4
y	18	10	4	0	−2	−2	0	4	10

25. a. For each equation, investigate the pattern of change in the
y-values as the x-values increase or decrease at a constant rate.
Describe the patterns you find.

$$y = 2x^2 \qquad y = 3x^2 \qquad y = \tfrac{1}{2}x^2 \qquad y = -2x^2$$

   b. Use what you discovered in part (a) to predict the pattern of
change for each of these equations.

$$y = 5x^2 \qquad y = -4x^2 \qquad y = \tfrac{1}{4}x^2 \qquad y = ax^2$$

26. Use the graph below.

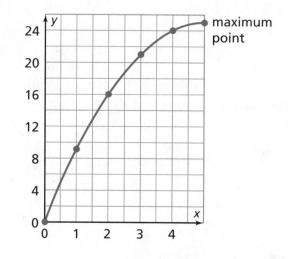

   a. Make a table of (x, y) values for the six points shown on the graph.

   b. The graph shows a quadratic function. Extend the graph to show
x-values from 5 to 10. Explain how you know your graph is correct.

27. The graph shows a quadratic function. Extend the graph to show
x-values from -4 to 0.

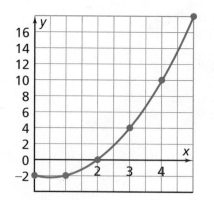

28. The table below shows a quadratic function. Extend the table to show *x*-values from 0 to −5. Explain how you know your table is correct.

x	y
0	8
1	3
2	0
3	−1
4	0
5	3

Connections

29. a. Make sketches that show two ways of completing the rectangle model below using whole numbers. For each sketch, express the area of the large rectangle in both expanded form and factored form.

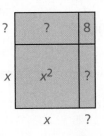

b. Is there more than one way to complete the rectangle model below using whole numbers? Explain.

30. Write two equivalent expressions for the area of the rectangle outlined in red below.

31. Consider these quadratic expressions.

$$2x^2 + 7x + 6 \qquad\qquad x^2 + 6x + 8$$

a. For each expression, sketch a rectangle whose area represents the expression. Which expression is easier to present in a rectangle model? Why?

b. Write each expression in factored form.

For Exercises 32–37, write the expression in expanded form.

32. $x(5 - x)$ **33.** $(x + 1)(x + 3)$ **34.** $(x - 1)(x + 3)$

35. $3x(x + 5)$ **36.** $(2x + 1)(x + 3)$ **37.** $(2x - 1)(x + 3)$

For Exercises 38–43, write the expression in factored form.

38. $x^2 - 9x + 8$ **39.** $4x^2 - 6x$ **40.** $3x^2 + 14x + 8$

41. $4x^2 + 6x$ **42.** $4x^2 - x - 3$ **43.** $x^3 - 2x^2 - 3x$

44. Min was having trouble factoring the expression in Exercise 40. Ricardo suggested that she use a rectangle model.

a. Explain how a rectangle model can help Min factor the expression. Make a sketch to illustrate your explanation.

b. How you can factor an expression without drawing a rectangle?

45. A diagonal of a polygon is a line segment connecting any two nonadjacent vertices. A quadrilateral has two diagonals like the one below.

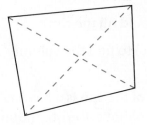

    a. How many diagonals does a pentagon have? How many does a hexagon have? A heptagon? An octagon?

    b. How many diagonals does an *n*-sided polygon have?

46. These "trains" are formed by joining identical squares.

Train 1   Train 2   Train 3   Train 4   Train 5

    a. How many rectangles are in each of the first five trains? For example, the diagram below shows the six rectangles in Train 3. (Remember, a square is a rectangle.)

    b. Make a table showing the number of rectangles in each of the first ten trains.

    c. How can you use the pattern of change in your table to find the number of rectangles in Train 15?

    d. Write an equation for the number of rectangles in Train *n*.

    e. Use your equation to find the number of rectangles in Train 15.

47. a. What is the area of the base of the can?

b. How many centimeter cubes or parts of cubes can fit in a single layer on the bottom of the can?

c. How many layers of this size would fill the can?

d. Use your answers to parts (a)–(c) to find the volume of the can.

e. The label on the lateral surface of the can is a rectangle with a height of 10 centimeters. What is the other dimension of the label?

f. What is the area of the label?

g. Use your answers to parts (a) and (f) to find the surface area of the can.

10 cm

10 cm

48. A company is trying to choose a box shape for a new product. It has narrowed the choices to the triangular prism and the cylinder shown below.

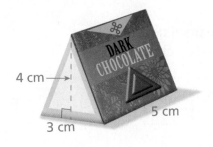

4 cm

3 cm

5 cm

4.24 cm

4.12 cm

a. Sketch a net for each box.

b. Find the surface area of each box.

c. Which box will require more cardboard to construct?

For Exercise 49–52, tell whether the pattern in each table represents a
function that is linear, quadratic, exponential, or none of these.

49.

x	y
0	2
3	4
5	5
6	6
7	7
8	8
10	10

50.

x	y
−3	12
−2	7
−1	4
0	3
1	4
2	7
3	12

51.

x	y
0	1
2	9
5	243
6	729
7	2,187
8	6,561
10	59,049

52.

x	y
1	−2
2	0
3	3
4	8
5	15
6	24
7	14

53. Multiple Choice Which equation represents a quadratic
relationship?

A. $y = (x − 1)(6 − 2)$

B. $y = 2x(3 − 2)$

C. $y = 2^x$

D. $y = x(x + 2)$

54. Multiple Choice Which equation has a graph with a minimum
point at $(1, 4)$?

F. $y = −x^2 + 5$

G. $y = −x^2 + 5x$

H. $y = x^2 − 2x + 5$

J. $y = −x^2 + 7x − 10$

55. Write each expression in expanded form.

a. $−3x(2x − 1)$

b. $1.5x(6 − 2x)$

Extensions

56. You can use Gauss's method to find the sum of the whole numbers from 1 to 10 by writing the sum twice as shown and adding vertically.

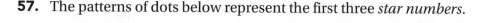

$$1 + 2 + 3 + 4 + 5 + 6 + 7 + 8 + 9 + 10$$
$$\underline{10 + 9 + 8 + 7 + 6 + 5 + 4 + 3 + 2 + 1}$$
$$11 + 11 + 11 + 11 + 11 + 11 + 11 + 11 + 11 + 11$$

Each vertical sum of 11 occurs 10 times, or $10(11) = 110$. This result is twice the sum of the numbers from 1 to 10, so you divide by 2 to get $\frac{10(11)}{2} = \frac{110}{5} = 55$.

a. How can you use this idea to find $1 + 2 + 3 + \ldots + 99 + 100$?

b. How could you use this idea to find $1 + 2 + 3 + \ldots + n$ for any whole number n?

c. How is this method related to Gauss's method?

57. The patterns of dots below represent the first three *star numbers*.

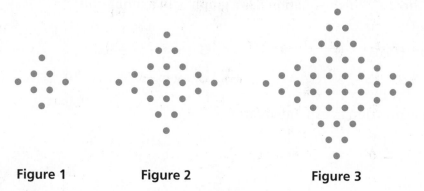

      Figure 1   **Figure 2**   **Figure 3**

a. What are the first three star numbers?

b. Find the next three star numbers.

c. Write an equation you could use to calculate the nth star number.

58. In parts (a) and (b), explain your answers by drawing pictures or writing a convincing argument.

a. Ten former classmates attend their class reunion. They all shake hands with each other. How many handshakes occur?

b. A little later, two more classmates arrive. Suppose these two people shake hands with each other and the ten other classmates. How many new handshakes occur?

59. The pattern of dots below represents the first three *hexagonal numbers*.

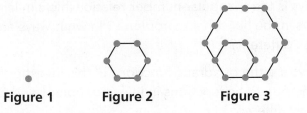

Figure 1   **Figure 2**   **Figure 3**

a. What are the first three hexagonal numbers?

b. Find the next two hexagonal numbers.

c. Write an equation you can use to calculate the *n*th hexagonal number.

60. There are 30 squares of various sizes in this 4-by-4 grid.

a. Sixteen of the squares are the identical small squares that make up the grid. Find the other 14 squares. Draw pictures or give a description.

b. How many squares are in an *n*-by-*n* grid? (**Hint:** Start with some simple cases and search for a pattern.)

61. Complete parts (a) and (b) for each equation.

$$y_1 = x + 1 \qquad\qquad y_2 = (x + 1)(x + 2)$$
$$y_3 = (x + 1)(x + 2)(x + 3) \qquad y_4 = (x + 1)(x + 2)(x + 3)(x + 4)$$

a. Describe the shape of the graph of the equation. Include any special features.

b. Describe the pattern of change between the variables.

In this Investigation, you counted handshakes and studied geometric patterns. You found that you can represent these situations with quadratic functions. The following questions will help you summarize what you have learned.

Think about these questions. Discuss your ideas with other students and your teacher. Then write a summary of your findings in your notebook.

1. **a.** In **what** ways is the triangular-number relationship similar to the relationships in the handshake problems? In what ways are these relationships different?

   b. In **what** ways are the quadratic functions in this Investigation similar to the quadratic functions in Investigations 1 and 2? In what ways are they different?

2. **a.** In a table of values for a quadratic function, **how** can you use the pattern of change to predict the next value?

   b. **How** can you use a table of values to decide if a function is quadratic?

3. **Compare** the patterns of change for linear, exponential, and quadratic functions.

Common Core Mathematical Practices

As you worked on the Problems in this Investigation, you used prior knowledge to make sense of them. You also applied Mathematical Practices to solve the Problems. Think back over your work, the ways you thought about the Problems, and how you used Mathematical Practices.

Ken described his thoughts in the following way:

A member of our group suggested that we could think of the triangular numbers as half of a rectangle with dimensions n and $n + 1$. He sketched diagrams to convince us that his reasoning was valid.

Another member of our group noticed that the first triangular number is 1. She explained that you add 2 to get the next triangular number. Then you add 3 to get the next number. You continue to add the next consecutive number to get the next triangular number. Both methods gave the same results for determining triangular numbers.

Common Core Standards for Mathematical Practice
MP2 Reason abstractly and quantitatively.

? • What other Mathematical Practices can you identify in Ken's reasoning?

• Describe a Mathematical Practice that you and your classmates used to solve a different Problem in this Investigation.

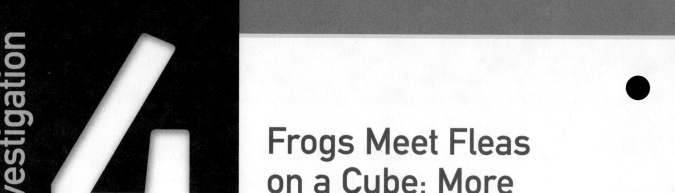
Frogs Meet Fleas on a Cube: More Applications of Quadratic Functions

When you make a snowboard jump, gravity pulls you toward Earth. When you throw or kick a ball into the air, gravity brings it back down. For several hundred years, scientists have used mathematical models to describe and predict the effect of gravity on the position, velocity, and acceleration of falling objects.

Common Core State Standards

A-REI.D.10 Understand that the graph of an equation in two variables is the set of all its solutions plotted in the coordinate plane, often forming a curve (which could be a line).

F-IF.B.4 For a function that models a relationship between two quantities, interpret key features of graphs and tables in terms of the quantities, and sketch graphs showing key features given a verbal description of the relationship.

F-IF.C.7 Graph functions expressed symbolically and show key features of the graph, by hand in simple cases and using technology for more complicated cases.

F-IF.C.7a Graph linear and quadratic functions and show intercepts, maxima, and minima.

Also A-CED.A.2, F-IF.C.9, F-LE.A.1, F-LE.A.1a, F-LE.A.1b

Did You Know?

Aristotle, the ancient Greek philosopher and scientist, believed that heavier objects fall faster than lighter objects. In the late 1500s, the great Italian scientist Galileo challenged this idea.

It is said that, while observing a hailstorm, Galileo noticed that large and small hailstones hit the ground at the same time. If Aristotle were correct, this would happen only if the larger stones dropped from a higher point or if the smaller stones started falling first. Galileo didn't think either of these explanations was probable.

A famous story claims that Galileo proved that heavy and light objects fall at the same rate by climbing to the highest point he could find—the top of the Tower of Pisa—and dropping two objects simultaneously. Although they had different weights, the objects hit the ground at the same time.

4.1 Tracking a Ball
Interpreting a Table and an Equation

No matter how hard you throw or kick a ball into the air, gravity returns it to Earth. In this Problem, you will explore how the height of a thrown ball changes over time.

Problem 4.1

Suppose you throw a ball straight up in the air. This table shows how the height of the ball might change over time as it goes up and then returns to the ground.

(A)
1. Describe how the height of the ball changes over this 4-second time period.

2. Without actually making the graph, describe what the graph of these data would look like. Include as many important features as you can.

3. Do you think these data represent a quadratic function? Explain.

(B) The height h of the ball in feet after t seconds can be described by the equation $h = -16t^2 + 64t$.

1. Graph this equation on your calculator.

2. Does the graph match the description you gave in Question A? Explain.

3. When does the ball reach a height of about 58 feet? Explain.

4. Use the equation to find the height of the ball after 1.6 seconds.

5. When will the ball reach the ground? Explain.

Height of Thrown Ball

Time (seconds)	Height (feet)
0.00	0
0.25	15
0.50	28
0.75	39
1.00	48
1.25	55
1.50	60
1.75	63
2.00	64
2.25	63
2.50	60
2.75	55
3.00	48
3.25	39
3.50	28
3.75	15
4.00	0

A C E Homework starts on page 80.

4.2 Measuring Jumps
Comparing Quadratic Functions

Many animals are known for their jumping abilities. Most frogs can jump several times their body length. Fleas are tiny, but they can easily leap onto a dog or a cat. Some humans have amazing jumping ability as well. Many professional basketball players have vertical leaps of more than 3 feet!

In Problem 4.1, the initial height of the ball is 0 feet. This is not very realistic because it means you would have to lie on the ground and release the ball without extending your arms. A more realistic equation for the height of the ball is $h = -16t^2 + 64t + 6$.

- Compare this equation with the equation in Problem 4.1.

- Use your calculator to make a table and a graph of this quadratic function.

- Compare your graph with the graph of the equation in Problem 4.1. Consider the following:

  - the maximum height reached by the ball

  - the x- and y-intercepts

  - the patterns of change in the height over time

- What information do the coefficients of t^2 and t, and the constant term, tell you about the graph of $h = -16t^2 + 64t + 6$?

Problem 4.2

A Suppose a frog, a flea, and a basketball player jump straight up. Their heights in feet after t seconds are modeled by these equations.

$$\text{Frog: } h = -16t^2 + 12t + 0.2$$
$$\text{Flea: } h = -16t^2 + 8t$$
$$\text{Basketball player: } h = -16t^2 + 16t + 6.5$$

1. Use your calculator to make tables and graphs of these three equations. Look at heights for time values between 0 seconds and 1 second. In your tables, use time intervals of 0.1 second.

2. What is the maximum height reached by each jumper? When is the maximum height reached?

3. How long does each jump last?

4. What do the **constant terms** 0.2 and 6.5 tell you about the frog and the basketball player? How is this information represented on the graph?

5. For each jumper, describe the pattern of change in the height over time. Explain how the pattern is reflected in the table and the graph.

B A jewelry maker would like to increase his profit by raising the price of his jade earrings. However, he knows that if he raises the price too high, he won't sell as many earrings and his profit will decrease.

The jewelry maker's business consultant develops the equation $P = 50s - s^2$ to predict the monthly profit P for a sales price s.

1. Make a table and a graph for this equation.

2. What do the equation, table, and graph suggest about the relationship between price and profit?

3. What price will bring the greatest profit?

4. How does this equation compare with the equations in Question A? How does it compare with other equations in this Unit?

A C E Homework starts on page 80.

Did You Know?

- The average flea weighs 0.000001 pound and is 2 to 3 millimeters long. It can pull 160,000 times its own weight and can jump 150 times its own length. This is equivalent to a human being pulling 24 million pounds and jumping nearly 1,000 feet!

- There are 3,000 known species and subspecies of fleas. Fleas are found on all land masses, including Antarctica.

- Most fleas make their homes on bats, rats, squirrels, and mice.

- The bubonic plague, which killed a quarter of Europe's population in the fourteenth century, was spread by rat fleas.

- Flea circuses originated about 300 years ago and were popular in the United States a century ago.

FLEA CIRCUS

4.3 Painted Cubes
Looking at Several Functions

Leon invents a puzzle. He makes a large cube from 1,000 centimeter cubes.

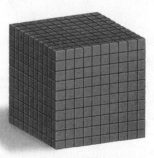

He paints the faces of the large cube. When the paint dries, he separates the puzzle into the original centimeter cubes. The object of Leon's puzzle is to reassemble the cubes so no unpainted faces are showing.

When Leon examines the centimeter cubes, he notices that some are painted on only one face, some on two faces, and some on three faces. Many aren't painted at all.

> **?** For any size of painted cube, what kind of equation tells you how many cubes will be painted on 1 face? 2 faces? 3 faces? 0 faces?

Problem 4.3

In this Problem, you will investigate smaller versions of Leon's puzzle.

A 1. The cube at the right is made of centimeter cubes. The faces of this cube are painted. Suppose you broke the cube into centimeter cubes. How many centimeter cubes would be painted on

    a. three faces?   **b.** two faces?

    c. one face?   **d.** no faces?

Problem **4.3**   *continued*

2. Answer the questions from part (1) for cubes with edges with lengths of 3, 4, 5, and 6 centimeters.

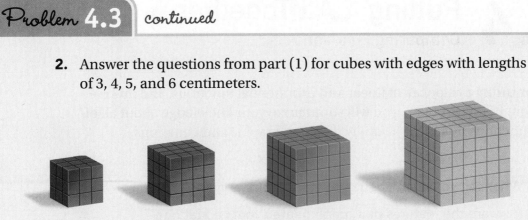

Organize your data in a table like the one below.

Edge Length of Large Cube	Number of Centimeter Cubes	Number of Centimeter Cubes Painted On			
		3 faces	**2 faces**	**1 face**	**0 faces**
2	■	■	■	■	■
3	■	■	■	■	■
4	■	■	■	■	■
5	■	■	■	■	■
6	■	■	■	■	■

B Study the patterns in the table.

1. Describe the relationship between the edge length of the large cube and the total number of centimeter cubes.

2. Describe the relationship between the edge length of the large cube and the number of centimeter cubes painted on

    a. three faces   **b.** two faces

    c. one face   **d.** zero faces

3. Decide whether each relationship in parts (1) and (2) is a linear function, quadratic function, exponential function, or none of these.

C **1.** Write an equation for each relationship in Question B. Tell what the variables and numbers in each equation mean.

2. Sketch the graph of each equation.

A C E Homework starts on page 80.

4.4 Putting It All Together
Comparing Functions

In prior Units, you looked at linear and exponential functions, and inverse variation. In this Problem, you will summarize your knowledge about all of these functions by sorting a variety of tables, graphs, and equations.

> (?) • What can you learn about a function from its graph?
>
> • How are the features of a graph related to its equation?
>
> • How can you determine if a function is linear, exponential, or quadratic?

Problem 4.4

For this Problem, you will be given some cards that have information about functions. Each card contains either an equation (E), a graph (G), function properties (P), or a table (T). Sort the cards into families that represent the same function. Then, complete Questions A–C for each family.

A Write a short summary about the family. Include as many details as you can.

B Make a new card that belongs to the family.

C Describe a problem that can be represented by the family.

A C E Homework starts on page 80.

$xy = 1$ E37	$y = x \cdot x^2$ E28	$y = 2^x$ E42
$y = (x + 2)^2$ E11	$y = x^2 + 4x + 4$ E35	$y = \frac{2}{1}x + 0$ E70

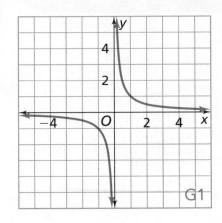

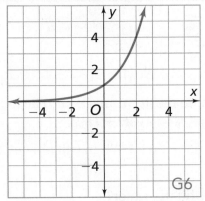

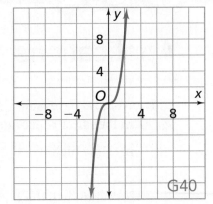

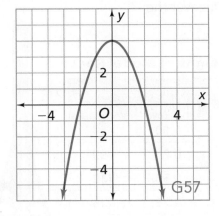

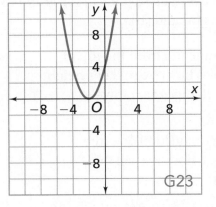

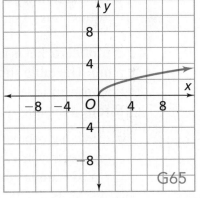

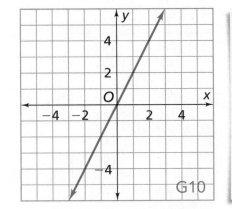

Function Properties
- No maximum value
- No minimum value
- No *x*-intercepts
- No *y*-intercept
- Symmetric about origin
- Not defined at *x* = 0 or *y* = 0

P49

Function Properties
- No maximum value
- Minimum value at *x* = 0
- One *x*-intercept
- *y*-intercept at 0
- No symmetry
- Not defined at *x* < 0

P17

x	y
−2	−8
−1	−1
0	0
1	1
2	8
3	27
	T64

x	y
−2	0
−1	3
0	4
1	3
2	0
3	−5
	T69

x	y
0.5	3.75
−0.5	3.75
−4	−12
4	−12
5	−21
−5	−21
	T21

x	y
1	2
2	4
4	8
8	16
16	32
32	64
	T46

x	y
1	1
25	5
100	10
$\frac{1}{4}$	$\frac{1}{2}$
0.01	0.1
	T29

x	y
−2	0.25
−1	0.5
0	1
1	2
2	4
3	8
	T18

Applications

1. A signal flare is fired into the air from a boat. The height h of the flare in feet after t seconds is $h = -16t^2 + 160t$.

   a. How high will the flare travel? When will it reach this maximum height?

   b. When will the flare hit the water?

   c. Explain how you could use a table and a graph to answer the questions in parts (a) and (b).

2. A model rocket is launched from the top of a hill. The table shows how the rocket's height above ground level changes as it travels through the air.

   a. How high above ground level does the rocket travel? When does it reach this maximum height?

   b. From what height is the rocket launched?

   c. How long does it take the rocket to return to the top of the hill?

Height of Model Rocket

Time (seconds)	Height (feet)
0.00	84
0.25	99
0.50	112
0.75	123
1.00	132
1.25	139
1.50	144
1.75	147
2.00	148
2.25	147
2.50	144
2.75	139
3.00	132
3.25	123
3.50	112
3.75	99
4.00	84

3. A basketball player throws the ball, attempting to make a basket. The graph shows the height of the ball starting when it leaves the player's hands.

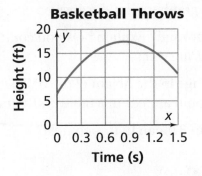

Basketball Throws

a. Estimate the height of the ball when the player releases it.

b. When does the ball reach its maximum height? What is the maximum height?

c. How long does it take the ball to reach the basket (a height of 10 feet)?

4. The highest dive in the Olympic Games is from a 10-meter platform. The height h in meters of a diver t seconds after leaving the platform can be estimated by the equation $h = 10 + 4.9t - 4.9t^2$.

a. Make a table of the relationship between time and height.

b. Sketch a graph of the relationship between time and height.

c. When will the diver hit the water's surface? How can you find this answer by using your graph? How can you find this answer by using your table?

d. When will the diver be 5 meters above the water?

e. When is the diver falling at the fastest rate? How is this shown in the table? How is this shown in the graph?

5. Kelsey jumps from a diving board, springing up into the air and then dropping feet-first. The distance d in feet from her feet to the pool's surface t seconds after she jumps is $d = -16t^2 + 18t + 10$.

a. What is the maximum height of Kelsey's feet during this jump? When does the maximum height occur?

b. When do Kelsey's feet hit the water?

c. What does the constant term 10 in the equation tell you about Kelsey's jump?

6. The equation $h = -16t^2 + 48t + 8$ describes how the height h of a ball in feet changes over time t.

 a. What is the maximum height reached by the ball? Explain how you could use a table and a graph to find the answer.

 b. When does the ball hit the ground? Explain how you could use a table and a graph to find the answer.

 c. Describe the pattern of change in the height of the ball over time. Explain how this pattern would appear in a table and a graph.

 d. What does the constant term 8 mean in this context?

For Exercises 7–10, complete parts (a)–(d).

 a. Sketch a graph of the equation.

 b. Find the x- and y-intercepts. Label these points on your graph.

 c. Draw and label the line of symmetry.

 d. Label the coordinates of the maximum or minimum point.

7. $y = 9 - x^2$ **8.** $y = 2x^2 - 4x$

9. $y = 6x - x^2$ **10.** $y = x^2 + 6x + 8$

11. a. How can you tell from a quadratic equation whether the graph will have a maximum point or a minimum point?

 b. How are the x- and y-intercepts of the graph of a quadratic function related to its equation?

 c. How are the x- and y-intercepts related to the line of symmetry?

For Exercises 12–17, predict the shape of the graph of the equation. Give the maximum or minimum point, the x-intercepts, and the line of symmetry. Use a graphing calculator to check your predictions.

12. $y = x^2$ **13.** $y = -x^2$ **14.** $y = x^2 + 1$

15. $y = x^2 + 6x + 9$ **16.** $y = x^2 - 2$ **17.** $y = x(4 - x)$

18. A cube with edges of length 12 centimeters is built from centimeter cubes. The faces of the large cube are painted. How many of the centimeter cubes will have

   a. three painted faces?   **b.** two painted faces?

   c. one painted face?   **d.** no painted faces?

19. Four large cubes are built from centimeter cubes. The faces of each large cube are painted. In parts (a)–(d), determine the size of the large cube. Then, tell how many of its centimeter cubes have 0, 1, 2, and 3 painted faces.

   a. For Cube A, 1,000 of the centimeter cubes have no painted faces.

   b. For Cube B, 864 of the centimeter cubes have one painted face.

   c. For Cube C, 132 of the centimeter cubes have two painted faces.

   d. For Cube D, 8 of the centimeter cubes have three painted faces.

20. **a.** Copy and complete each table. Describe the pattern of change.

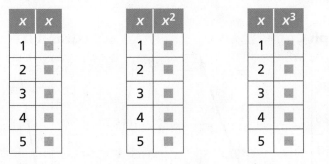

x	x
1	▦
2	▦
3	▦
4	▦
5	▦

x	x^2
1	▦
2	▦
3	▦
4	▦
5	▦

x	x^3
1	▦
2	▦
3	▦
4	▦
5	▦

   b. For each table, tell which column in the painted-cubes table in Problem 4.3 has a similar pattern. Explain.

21. Consider the functions described by these equations. Are any of them similar to functions in the painted-cubes situation? Explain.

$$y_1 = 2(x - 1) \qquad y_2 = (x - 1)^3 \qquad y_3 = 4(x - 1)^2$$

For Exercises 22–25, match the equation with its graph. Then, give the line of symmetry for each graph and explain how to locate it.

22. $y = (x + 7)(x + 2)$

23. $y = x(x + 3)$

24. $y = (x - 4)(x + 6)$

25. $y = (x - 5)(x + 5)$

Graph A

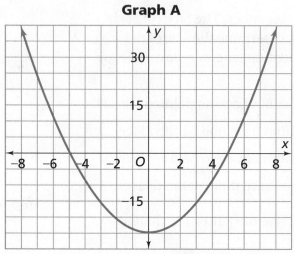

Graph B

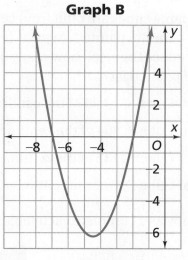

Graph C

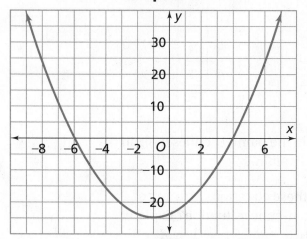

Graph D

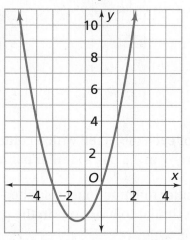

26. **a.** How are the graphs at the right similar?

    b. How are the graphs different?

    c. The maximum value for $y = x(10 - x)$ occurs when $x = 5$. How can you find the y-coordinate of the maximum value?

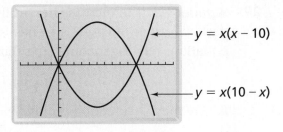

$y = x(x - 10)$

$y = x(10 - x)$

    d. The minimum value for $y = x(x - 10)$ occurs when $x = 5$. How can you find the y-coordinate of the minimum value?

27. **Multiple Choice** Which quadratic equation has x-intercepts at $(3, 0)$ and $(-1, 0)$?

    A. $y = x^2 - 1x + 3$ **B.** $y = x^2 - 2x + 3$ **C.** $y = 3x^2 - 1x$ **D.** $y = x^2 - 2x - 3$

Connections

28. **a.** Describe the patterns of change in each table. (Look closely. You may find more than one.) Explain how you can use the patterns to find the missing entry.

Table 1	
x	y
0	25
1	50
2	100
3	200
4	400
5	■

Table 2	
x	y
−3	3
−2	6
−1	9
0	12
1	15
2	■

Table 3	
x	y
2	6
3	12
4	20
5	30
6	42
7	■

Table 4	
x	y
−2	21
−1	24
0	25
1	24
2	21
3	■

    b. Tell which equation matches each table.

$$y_1 = x^2 - 12 \qquad y_2 = x(x + 1) \qquad y_3 = 25 - x^2$$

$$y_4 = (x)(x)(x) \qquad y_5 = 3(x + 4) \qquad y_6 = 25(2)^x$$

    c. Which tables represent quadratic functions? Explain.

    d. Do any of the tables include the maximum y-value for the relationship?

    e. Do any of the tables include the minimum y-value for the relationship?

29. A potter wants to increase her profits by changing the price of a particular style of vase. Using past sales data, she writes these two equations relating income *I* to selling price *p*:

$$I = (100 - p)p \text{ and } I = 100p - p^2$$

a. Are the two equations equivalent? Explain.

b. Show that $I = 100 - p^2$ is not equivalent to the original equations.

c. It costs $350 to rent a booth at a craft fair. The potter's profit for the fair will be her income minus the cost of the booth. Write an equation for the profit *M* as a function of the price *p*.

d. What price would give the maximum profit? What will the maximum profit be?

e. For what prices will there be a profit rather than a loss?

30. Eggs are often sold by the dozen. When farmers send eggs to supermarkets, they often stack the eggs in bigger containers that are 12 eggs long, 12 eggs wide, and 12 eggs high.

a. How many eggs are in each layer of the container?

b. How many eggs are there in an entire container?

31. A square has sides of length x.

   a. Write formulas for the area A and perimeter P of the square in terms of x.

   b. Suppose the side lengths of the square are doubled. How do the area and perimeter change?

   c. How do the area and perimeter change if the side lengths are tripled?

   d. What is the perimeter of a square if its area is 36 square meters?

   e. Make a table of side length, perimeter, and area values for squares with whole-number side lengths from 0 to 12.

   f. Sketch graphs of the data (*side length, area*) and (*side length, perimeter*) from your table.

   g. Tell whether the patterns of change in the tables and graphs suggest linear, quadratic, or exponential functions, or none of these. Explain.

32. A cube has edges of length x.

   a. Write a formula for the volume V of the cube in terms of x.

   b. Suppose the edge lengths of the cube double. How does the volume change?

   c. How does the surface area and volume change if the edge lengths triple?

   d. Make a table for cubes with whole-number edge lengths from 0 to 12. Title the columns "Side Length," "Surface Area," and "Volume."

   e. Sketch graphs of the data (*edge length, surface area*) and (*edge length, volume*) from your table.

   f. Tell whether the patterns of change in the tables and graphs suggest linear, quadratic, or exponential functions, or none of these.

33. a. Find the areas of these circles.

2 cm

1 cm

b. Copy and complete this table. Is the relationship between the area and the radius quadratic? Explain.

Radius (cm)	1	2	3	4	x
Area (cm²)	■	■	■	■	■

c. Below are nets for two cylinders with heights of 2 meters. Find the surface areas of the cylinders.

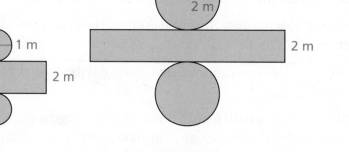

1 m
2 m
2 m
2 m

d. Copy and complete this table. Is the relationship between the surface area and the radius quadratic? Explain.

Radius (m)	1	2	3	4	x
Height (m)	2	2	2	2	2
Surface Area (m²)	■	■	■	■	■

34. Multiple Choice The equation $h = 4 + 63t - 16t^2$ represents the height h of a baseball in feet t seconds after it is hit. After how many seconds will the ball hit the ground?

A. 2 seconds   **B.** 4 seconds   **C.** 5 seconds   **D.** 15 seconds

35. a. Copy and complete the table to show surface areas of cylinders with equal radius and height. Use the nets shown.

Radius (ft)	1	2	3	4	x
Height (ft)	1	2	3	4	x
Surface Area (ft²)	■	■	■	■	■

b. Is the relationship between surface area and radius a quadratic function? Explain.

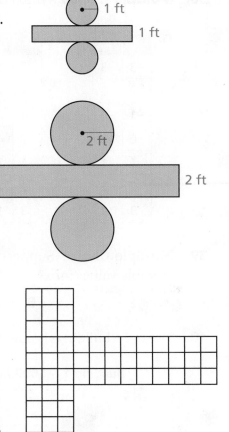

36. At the right is a net of a cube, divided into square units.

a. What is the edge length of the cube?

b. Find the surface area and volume of the cube.

c. Draw a net for a cube with a volume of 64 cubic units. What is the length of each edge of the cube? What is the surface area of the cube?

d. What formula relates the edge length of a cube to its volume? Is this relationship a quadratic function? Explain.

37. Silvio wants to gift wrap the cubic box shown. He has 10 square feet of wrapping paper. Is this enough to wrap the gift? Explain.

16 in.

38. Multiple Choice Which table could represent a quadratic function?

F.

x	y
−3	−3
−2	−2
−1	−1
0	0
1	1
2	2
3	3

G.

x	y
−3	1
−2	2
−1	3
0	4
1	3
2	2
3	1

H.

x	y
1	0
2	2
3	6
4	12
5	20
6	30
7	42

J.

x	y
−1	10
0	7
1	4
2	1
3	4
4	7
5	10

39. Multiple Choice Suppose $y = x^2 - 4x$ and $y = 0$. What are all the possible values for x?

A. −4   **B.** 0   **C.** 4 or 0   **D.** −4 or 0

40. The cube buildings below are shown from the front right corner.

Building 1   Building 2   Building 3   Building 4

These drawings show the base outline, front view, and right view of Building 1. Draw these views for the other three buildings.

Base outline   Front view   Right view

41. Below are three views of a cube building. Draw a building that has all three views and has the greatest number of cubes possible. You may want to use isometric dot paper.

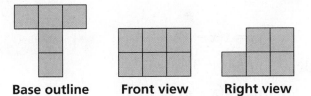

Base outline   **Front view**   **Right view**

42. Below are base plans for cube buildings. A *base plan* shows the shape of the building's base and the number of cubes in each stack.

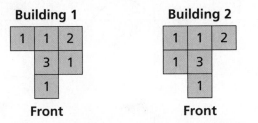

Make a drawing of each building from the front right corner. You may want to use isometric dot paper.

For Exercises 43–46, evaluate the expression for the given values of *x*.

43. $x(x-5)$ for $x = 5$ and $x = -5$

44. $3x^2 - x$ for $x = 1$ and $x = \frac{1}{3}$

45. $x^2 + 5x + 4$ for $x = 2$ and $x = -4$

46. $(x-7)(x+2)$ for $x = -2$ and $x = 2$

47. Match the equations, graphs, and properties. Each equation is given in factored form. The window of the graphs is shown at the right.

WINDOW   FORMAT
 Xmin=−5
 Xmax=5
 Xscl=1
 Ymin=−10
 Ymax=10
 Yscl=1
 Xres=1

Equations:

$$y_1 = x^2$$

$$y_2 = x(x - 4)$$

$$y_3 = (x + 3)(x - 3)$$

$$y_4 = (x + 3)(x + 3)$$

$$y_5 = x(4 - x)$$

$$y_6 = x(x + 4)$$

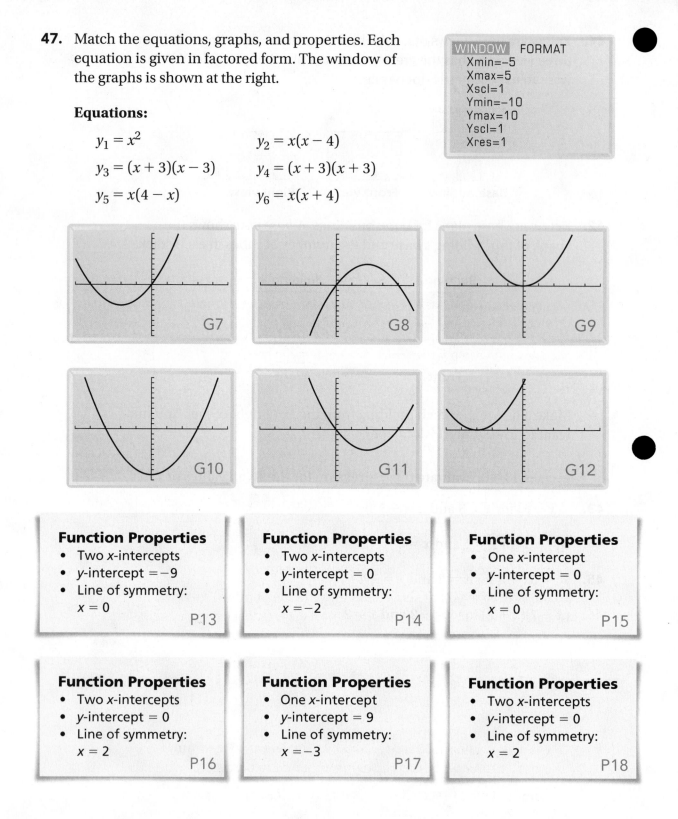

G7

G8

G9

G10

G11

G12

Function Properties
- Two x-intercepts
- y-intercept $= -9$
- Line of symmetry: $x = 0$

P13

Function Properties
- Two x-intercepts
- y-intercept $= 0$
- Line of symmetry: $x = -2$

P14

Function Properties
- One x-intercept
- y-intercept $= 0$
- Line of symmetry: $x = 0$

P15

Function Properties
- Two x-intercepts
- y-intercept $= 0$
- Line of symmetry: $x = 2$

P16

Function Properties
- One x-intercept
- y-intercept $= 9$
- Line of symmetry: $x = -3$

P17

Function Properties
- Two x-intercepts
- y-intercept $= 0$
- Line of symmetry: $x = 2$

P18

48. Refer to Graphs G7 and G8 from Exercise 47. Without using your calculator, answer the following questions.

    a. Suppose parabola G7 is shifted 1 unit left. Write an equation for this new parabola.

    b. Suppose parabola G7 is shifted 4 units right. Write an equation for this new parabola.

    c. Can parabola G7 be transformed into parabola G8 by a shift to the right only? Explain.

Extensions

49. A puzzle involves a strip of seven squares, three pennies, and three nickels. The starting setup is shown.

To solve the puzzle, you must switch the positions of the coins so the nickels are on the left and the pennies are on the right. You can move a coin to an empty square by sliding it or by jumping it over one coin. You can move pennies only to the right and nickels only to the left.

You can make variations of this puzzle by changing the numbers of coins and the length of the strip. Each puzzle should have the same number of each type of coin and one empty square.

    a. Make drawings that show each move (slide or jump) required to solve puzzles with 1, 2, and 3 coins of each type. How many moves does it take to solve each puzzle?

    b. A puzzle with n nickels and n pennies can be solved with $n^2 + 2n$ moves. Use this expression to calculate the number of moves required to solve puzzles with 1, 2, 3, 4, 5, 6, 7, 8, 9, and 10 of each type of coin.

    c. Do your calculations for 1, 2, and 3 coins of each type from part (b) agree with the numbers you found in part (a)?

    d. By calculating first and second differences in the data from part (b), verify that the relationship between the number of moves and the number of each type of coin is quadratic.

Use the following information for Exercises 50–52.

A soccer coach wants to take her 20-player team to the state capital for a tournament. A travel company is organizing the trip. The cost will be $125 per student. The coach thinks this is too expensive, so she decides to invite other students to go along. For each extra student, the cost of the trip will be reduced by $1 per student.

50. The travel company's expenses for the trip are $75 per student. The remaining money is profit. What will the company's profit be if the following numbers of students go on the trip?

a. 20   b. 25   c. 60   d. 80

51. Let n represent the number of students who go on the trip. In parts (a)–(d), write an equation for the relationship described. It may help to make a table like the one shown here.

State Capital Trip

Number of Students	Price per Student	Travel Company's Income	Travel Company's Expenses	Travel Company's Profit
20	$125	20 × $125 = $2,500	20 × $75 = $1,500	$2,500 – $1,500 = $1,000
21	$124	■	■	■

a. the relationship between *the price per student* and n

b. the relationship between *the travel company's income* and n

c. the relationship between *the travel company's expenses* and n

d. the relationship between *the travel company's profit* and n

52. Use a calculator to make a table and a graph of the equation for the travel company's profit. Study the pattern of change in the profit as the number of students increases from 25 to 75.

a. What number of students gives the company the maximum profit?

b. What numbers of students guarantee the company will earn a profit?

c. What numbers of students will give the company a profit of at least $1,200?

53. The Terryton Tile Company makes floor tiles. One tile design uses grids of small, colored squares as in this 4 × 4 pattern.

   a. Suppose you apply the same design rule to a 5 × 5 pattern. How many small squares will be blue? How many will be yellow? How many will be red?

   b. How many small squares of each color will there be if you apply the rule to a 10 × 10 pattern?

   c. How many small squares of each color will there be if you apply the rule to an *n* × *n* pattern?

   d. What kinds of relationships between the side length of the pattern and the number of small squares of each color do the expressions in part (c) describe? Explain.

54. This prism is made from centimeter cubes. After the prism was built, its faces were painted. How many centimeter cubes have

   a. no painted faces?   **b.** one painted face?

   c. two painted faces?   **d.** three painted faces?

   e. How many centimeter cubes are there in all?

In this Investigation, you explored the relationship between height and time for several situations. You also looked for common features in the tables, graphs, and equations of quadratic functions. These questions will help you summarize what you have learned.

Think about these questions. Discuss your ideas with other students and your teacher. Then write a summary of your findings in your notebook.

1. **Describe** three real-world situations that can be modeled by quadratic functions. For each situation, give examples of questions that quadratic representations help to answer.

2. **How** can you recognize a quadratic function from

   a. a table?

   b. a graph?

   c. an equation?

3. **What** clues in a problem situation indicate that a linear, exponential, or quadratic function is an appropriate model for the data in the problem?

Common Core Mathematical Practices

As you worked on the Problems in this Investigation, you used prior knowledge to make sense of them. You also applied Mathematical Practices to solve the Problems. Think back over your work, the ways you thought about the Problems, and how you used Mathematical Practices.

Sophie described her thoughts in the following way:

In Problem 4.3, Zane noticed that the number of painted faces of the cube represents the surface area of the cube. Hank did not think this was true since the surface area of a cube is $6n^2$, where n is the side length of the cube.

Some of us knew that we could prove that Zane's conjecture is true if we could show that the surface area equals the sum of the algebraic expressions for the number of painted faces. This means that $6n^2 = 8(3) + 12(n - 2)(2) + 6(n - 2)^2(1)$. We were able to use what we learned in this Unit to show that this is true.

Common Core Standards for Mathematical Practice

MP3 Construct viable arguments and critique the reasoning of others.

? • What other Mathematical Practices can you identify in Sophie's reasoning?

• Describe a Mathematical Practice that you and your classmates used to solve a different Problem in this Investigation.

In this Unit, you studied quadratic functions. You learned to recognize quadratic patterns in graphs and tables and to write equations for those patterns. You answered questions about quadratic functions by solving equations and by finding maximum and minimum points on graphs.

Use Your Understanding: Algebraic Reasoning

Test your understanding and skill in working with quadratic relationships by solving these problems about a carnival.

1. In the game pictured at the right, players hit the end of a lever with a mallet, propelling a weight upward. The player wins a prize if the weight hits the bell at the top.

   The height h (in feet) of the weight t seconds after the mallet is struck is given by the equation $h = -16t^2 + bt$. The value of b depends on how hard the mallet hits the lever.

   a. Sketch the general shape of a graph of an equation of the form $h = -16t^2 + bt$.

   b. When Naomi plays, the weight rises 9 feet and falls back to the bottom in 1.5 seconds. Which table better matches this situation?

Table 1

Time (seconds)	0.0	0.25	0.5	0.75	1.0	1.25	1.5
Height (feet)	0	5	8	9	8	5	0

Table 2

Time (seconds)	0.0	0.25	0.5	0.75	1.0	1.25	1.5
Height (feet)	0	3	6	9	6	3	0

2. Wan's hit is just hard enough to cause the weight to touch the bell. This situation is modeled by $h = -16t^2 + 32t$.

   a. How high did the weight go?

   b. How long did it take the weight to return to the starting position?

   c. When was the weight 12 feet above the starting position?

3. The carnival is adding pony rides for young children. They have 180 feet of fence to build a rectangular pony corral.

   a. Let x represent the length of the pony corral in feet. Write an expression for the width in terms of x.

   b. Write an equation that shows how the area A of the corral is related to its length x.

   c. What length and width will give an area of 2,000 square feet? Write and solve an equation whose solution is the required length.

   d. What length and width will give the maximum area? Explain how you could use a table or graph to find this maximum area.

Explain Your Reasoning

To solve Problems 1–3, you used your knowledge of quadratic functions and of tables, graphs, and equations for quadratic situations.

4. Suppose the relationship between x and y is a quadratic function. What patterns would you expect to see
   a. in a table of (x, y) pairs?
   b. in a graph of (x, y) pairs?
   c. in an equation relating x and y?

5. How are the equations, tables, and graphs for quadratic relationships different from those for
   a. linear relationships?
   b. exponential relationships?

6. How can you tell whether the graph of a quadratic equation of the form $y = ax^2 + bx + c$ will have a maximum point or a minimum point?

7. What strategies can you use to solve quadratic equations such as $3x^2 - 5x + 3 = 0$ and $x^2 + 4x = 7$ by using
   a. a table of a quadratic function?
   b. a graph of a quadratic function?

English / Spanish Glossary

B **binomial** An algebraic expression that is the sum or difference of two terms. The expression $2x + 4$ is a binomial.

binomio Expresión algebraica que es la suma o diferencia de dos términos. La expresión $2x + 4$ es un binomio.

C **constant term** A number in an algebraic expression that is not multiplied by a variable. In the expanded form of a quadratic expression, $ax^2 + bx + c$, the constant term is the number c. The constant term in the expression $-16t^2 + 64t + 7$ is 7. The constant term in the expression $x^2 - 4$ is -4.

término constante Un número en una expresión algebraica que no está multiplicado por una variable. En la forma desarrollada de una expresión cuadrática, $ax^2 + bx + c$, el término constante es el número c. El término constante en la expresión $-16t^2 + 64t + 7$ es 7. El término constante en la expresión $x^2 - 4$ es -4.

D **dependent variable** One of the two variables in a relationship. Its value depends upon or is determined by the other variable called the *independent variable*. For example, the distance you travel on a car trip (dependent variable) depends on how long you drive (independent variable).

variable dependiente Una de las dos variables de una relación. Su valor depende o está determinado por el valor de la otra variable, llamada *variable independiente*. Por ejemplo, la distancia que recorres durante un viaje en carro (variable dependiente) depende de cuánto conduces (variable independiente).

describe Academic Vocabulary
To explain or tell in detail. A written description can contain facts and other information needed to communicate your answer. A diagram or a graph may also be included.

related terms *express, explain, illustrate*

sample Describe the graph of the equation $y = x^2 + 2x$.

The graph of $y = x^2 + 2x$ is a parabola that opens up. The minimum is located at $(-1, -1)$. The y-intercept and one of the x-intercepts is at the origin. The other x-intercept is located at $(-2, 0)$.

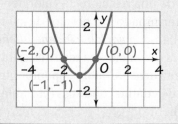

describir Vocabulario académico
Explicar o decir con detalle. Una descripción escrita puede contener datos y otra información necesaria para comunicar tu respuesta. También se puede incluir un diagrama o una gráfica.

términos relacionados *expresar, explicar, ilustrar*

ejemplo Describe la gráfica de la ecuación $y = x^2 + 2x$.

La gráfica de $y = x^2 + 2x$ es una parábola que se abre hacia arriba. El punto mínimo se localiza en $(-1, -1)$. El intercepto en y uno de los interceptos en x están en el origen. El otro intercepto en x se localiza en $(-2, 0)$.

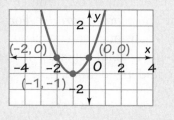

difference of squares An expression of the form $a^2 - b^2$. It can be factored as $(a + b)(a - b)$.

diferencia de cuadrados Una expresión de la forma $a^2 - b^2$. Se puede descomponer en factores de esta manera: $(a + b)(a - b)$.

Distributive Property For any three numbers a, b, and c, $a(b + c) = ab + ac$.

Propiedad distributiva Para tres números cualesquiera a, b y c, $a(b + c) = ab + ac$.

E **expanded form** The form of an expression composed of sums and differences of terms, rather than products of factors. The expressions $x^2 + 7x - 12$ and $x^2 + 2x$ are in expanded form.

forma desarrollada La forma de una expresión compuesta de sumas o diferencias de términos, en lugar de productos de factores. Las expresiones $x^2 + 7x - 12$ y $x^2 + 2x$ están representadas en forma desarrollada.

explain Academic Vocabulary
To give facts and details that make an idea easier to understand. Explaining something can involve a written summary supported by a diagram, chart, table, or any combination of these.

explicar Vocabulario académico
Dar datos y detalles que hacen que una idea sea más fácil de comprender. Explicar puede implicar un resumen escrito apoyado por un diagrama, una gráfica, una tabla o una combinación de estos.

related terms *clarify, justify, tell*

términos relacionados *aclarar, justificar, decir*

sample Darla factored the expression $x^2 + 15x + 56$. Explain what she did.

$$x^2 + 15x + 56 = x^2 + 7x + 8x + 56 \quad (1)$$
$$= x(x + 7) + 8(x + 7) \quad (2)$$
$$= (x + 8)(x + 7) \quad (3)$$

ejemplo Dora descompuso en factores la expresión $x^2 + 15x + 56$. Explica lo que hizo.

$$x^2 + 15x + 56 = x^2 + 7x + 8x + 56 \quad (1)$$
$$= x(x + 7) + 8(x + 7) \quad (2)$$
$$= (x + 8)(x + 7) \quad (3)$$

In Step 1, she rewrote 15x as the sum of 7x and 8x. In Step 2, she factored x from the first two terms and 8 from the last two terms. In Step 3, she factored (x + 7) from both terms.

En el Paso 1, volvió a escribir 15x como la suma de 7x y 8x. En el Paso 2, separó x como factor de los primeros dos términos y 8 de los últimos dos términos. En el Paso 3, separó (x + 7) de ambos términos.

F **factored form** The form of an expression composed of products of factors, rather than sums or differences of terms. The expressions $x(x - 2)$ and $(x + 3)(x + 4)$ are in factored form.

forma factorizada La forma de una expresión compuesta de productos de factores, en lugar de sumas o diferencias de términos. Las expresiones $x(x - 2)$ y $(x + 3)(x + 4)$ están representadas en forma factorizada.

independent variable One of the two variables in a relationship. Its value determines the value of the other variable called the *dependent variable*. If you organize a bike tour, for example, the number of people who register to go (independent variable) determines the cost for renting bikes (dependent variable).

variable independiente Una de las dos variables en una relación. Su valor determina el de la otra variable, llamada *variable dependiente*. Por ejemplo, si organizas un recorrido en bicicleta, el número de personas inscritas (variable independiente) determina el costo del alquiler de las bicicletas (variable dependiente).

like terms Terms with the same variable raised to the same power. In the expression $4x^2 + 3x - 2x^2 - 2x + 1$, $3x$ and $-2x$ are like terms, and $4x^2$ and $-2x^2$ are like terms.

términos semejantes Términos con la misma variable elevada a la misma potencia. En la expresión $4x^2 + 3x - 2x^2 - 2x + 1$, $3x$ y $-2x$ son términos semejantes, y $4x^2$ y $-2x^2$ también son términos semejantes.

line of symmetry A line that divides a graph or drawing into two halves that are mirror images of each other.

eje de simetría Recta que divide una gráfica o un dibujo en dos mitades en la que una es el reflejo de la otra.

linear term A part of an algebraic expression in expanded form in which the variable is raised to the first power. In the expression $4x^2 + 3x - 2x + 1$, $3x$ and $-2x$ are linear terms.

término lineal La parte de una expresión algebraica en forma desarrollada, en la que la variable está elevada a la primera potencia. En la expresión $4x^2 + 3x - 2x + 1$, $3x$ y $-2x$ son términos lineales.

maximum value of a function The greatest y-value of a function. If y is the height of a thrown object, then the maximum value of the height is the highest point the object reaches. If you throw a ball into the air, its height increases until it reaches the maximum height, and then its height decreases as it falls back to the ground. If y is the area of a rectangle with a fixed perimeter, then the maximum value of the area, or simply the maximum area, is the greatest area possible for a rectangle with that perimeter. In this Unit, you found that the maximum area for a rectangle with a perimeter of 20 meters is 25 square meters.

valor máximo de una función El mayor valor de y en una función. Si y es la altura de un objeto lanzado, entonces el valor máximo de la altura es la altura mayor que alcanza el objeto. Si lanzas una pelota al aire, su altura aumenta hasta que alcanza la altura máxima, y luego su altura disminuye a medida que cae hacia el suelo. Si y es el área de un rectángulo con un perímetro fijo, entonces el valor máximo del área, o simplemente el área máxima, es la mayor área posible para un rectángulo con ese perímetro. En esta unidad, estudiaste que el área máxima de un rectángulo con un perímetro de 20 metros es 25 metros cuadrados.

minimum value of a function The least *y*-value of a function. If *y* is the cost of an item, then the minimum value of the cost, or simply the minimum cost, is the least cost possible for the item.

valor mínimo de una función El valor menor de y en una función. Si y es el costo de un artículo, entonces el valor mínimo del costo, o simplemente el costo mínimo, es el menor costo posible para ese artículo.

P **parabola** The graph of a quadratic function. A parabola has a line of symmetry that passes through the maximum point if the graph opens downward or through the minimum point if the graph opens upward.

parábola La gráfica de una función cuadrática. Una parábola tiene un eje de simetría que pasa por el punto máximo si la gráfica se abre hacia abajo, o por el punto mínimo si la gráfica se abre hacia arriba.

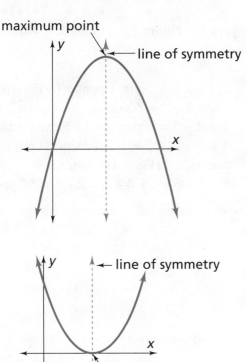

maximum point — line of symmetry

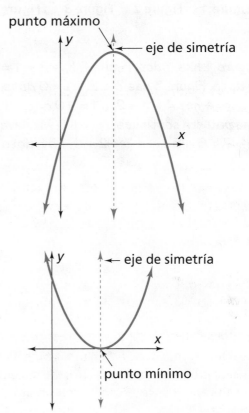

punto máximo — eje de simetría

line of symmetry

minimum point

eje de simetría

punto mínimo

predict Academic Vocabulary
To make an educated guess based on the analysis of real data.

related terms *estimate, guess, expect*

sample Predict how many dots will be in Figure 8.

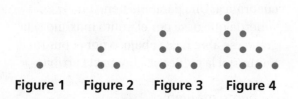

Figure 1 **Figure 2** **Figure 3** **Figure 4**

Figure 1 has 1 dot. Figure 2 has 2 + 1 = 3 dots. Figure 3 has 3 + 2 + 1 = 6 dots. Figure 4 has 4 + 3 + 2 + 1 = 10 dots. If the pattern continues, Figure 8 will have 8 + 7 + 6 + 5 + 4 + 3 + 2 + 1 = 36 dots.

predecir Vocabulario académico
Hacer una suposición basada en el análisis de datos reales.

términos relacionados *estimar, conjeturar, esperar*

ejemplo Predice cuántos puntos habrá en la Figura 8.

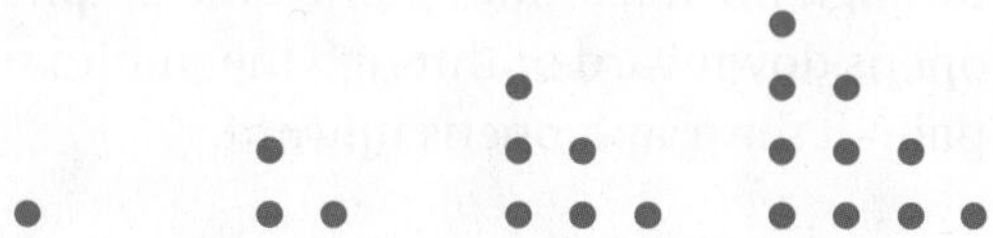

Figura 1 **Figura 2** **Figura 3** **Figura 4**

La Figura 1 tiene 1 punto. La Figura 2 tiene 2 + 1 = 3 puntos. La Figura 3 tiene 3 + 2 + 1 = 6 puntos. La Figura 4 tiene 4 + 3 + 2 + 1 = 10 puntos. Si el patrón continúa, la Figura 8 tendrá 8 + 7 + 6 + 5 + 4 + 3 + 2 + 1 = 36 puntos.

Frogs, Fleas, and Painted Cubes

quadratic expression An expression that is equivalent to an expression of the form $ax^2 + bx + c$, where a, b, and c are numbers and $a \neq 0$. An expression in factored form is quadratic if it has exactly two linear factors, each with the variable raised to the first power. An expression in expanded form is quadratic if the highest power of the variable is 2. For example, $2x^2$, $3x^2 - 2x$, and $4x^2 + 2x - 7$ are all quadratic expressions. The expression $x(x - 2)$ is also a quadratic expression because $x(x - 2) = x^2 - 2x$. In this Unit, you used quadratic expressions to represent areas of rectangles for a fixed perimeter, the number of high fives between members of a team, and the path of a ball thrown into the air.

expresión cuadrática Una expresión que es equivalente a una expresión de la forma $ax^2 + bx + c$, donde a, b, y c son números y $a \neq 0$. Una expresión en forma factorizada es cuadrática si tiene exactamente dos factores lineales, cada uno con la variable elevada a la primera potencia. Una expresión en forma desarrollada es cuadrática si la potencia mayor de la variable es 2. Por ejemplo, $2x^2$, $3x^2 - 2x$, y $4x^2 + 2x - 7$ son expresiones cuadráticas. La expresión $x(x - 2)$ también es una expresión cuadrática porque $x(x - 2) = x^2 - 2x$. En esta unidad, usaste expresiones cuadráticas para representar áreas de rectángulos con un perímetro fijo, el número de saludos entre los miembros de un equipo y el recorrido de una pelota que se lanza al aire.

quadratic function A function between independent and dependent variables such that, as the dependent values increase by a constant amount, the successive (first) differences between the dependent values change by a constant amount. For example, in $y = x^2$, when x increases by 1, the first differences for y are 3, 5, 7, 9, . . . and then the second differences are 2, 2, 2, . . . The graphs of quadratic functions have the shape of a ∪ or upside down ∪ with a line of symmetry through a maximum or minimum point on the graph that is perpendicular to the x-axis.

función cuadrática La función entre las variables dependiente e independiente de modo que, a medida que aumentan los valores de la variable dependiente en una cantidad constante, las (primeras) diferencias sucesivas entre los valores dependientes cambian en una cantidad constante. Por ejemplo, en $y = x^2$, a medida que x aumenta en 1, las primeras diferencias para y son 3, 5, 7, 9, . . . y las segundas diferencias son 2, 2, 2, . . . Las gráficas de las funciones cuadráticas tienen forma de ∪ o ∪ invertida, con un eje de simetría que pasa por el punto máximo o el punto mínimo de la gráfica que es perpendicular al eje de las x.

quadratic term A part of an expression in expanded form in which the variable is raised to the second power. In the expression $4x^2 + 3x - 2x^2 - 2x + 1$, $4x^2$ and $-2x^2$ are quadratic terms.

término cuadrático Parte de una expresión en forma desarrollada en la que la variable está elevada a la segunda potencia. En la expresión $4x^2 + 3x - 2x^2 - 2x + 1$, $4x^2$ y $-2x^2$ son términos cuadráticos.

S

sketch Academic Vocabulary

To draw a rough outline of something. When a sketch is asked for, it means that a drawing needs to be included in your response.

related terms *draw, illustrate*

sample The equation of the area of a rectangle is $A = w(20 - w)$, where w is the width of the rectangle in inches. Sketch a rectangle to represent the situation.

Label one side of the rectangle *w* inches and the other side 20 – *w* inches.

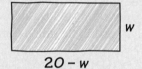

I sketched a graph of A = w(20 – w) to show all of the possible areas of the rectangle.

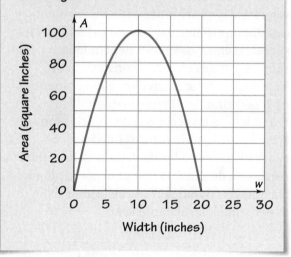

hacer un bosquejo Vocabulario académico

Dibujar un esbozo de algo. Cuando se pide un bosquejo, quiere decir que se debe incluir un dibujo en la respuesta.

términos relacionados *dibujar, ilustrar*

ejemplo La ecuación del área de un rectángulo es $A = a(20 - a)$, donde a es el ancho del rectángulo en pulgadas. Haz un bosquejo de un rectángulo y una gráfica para representar la situación.

Rotulo un lado del rectángulo a pulgads y el otro lado 20 – a pulgadas.

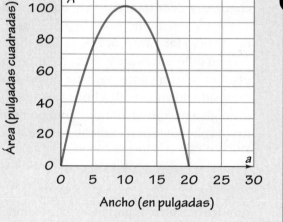

Hice el bosquejo de una gráfica de A = a(20 – a) para mostrár todas las áreas posibles del rectángulo.

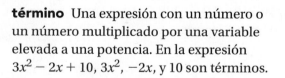

T

term An expression that consists of either a number or a number multiplied by a variable raised to a power. In the expression $3x^2 - 2x + 10$, $3x^2$, $-2x$, and 10 are terms.

término Una expresión con un número o un número multiplicado por una variable elevada a una potencia. En la expresión $3x^2 - 2x + 10$, $3x^2$, $-2x$, y 10 son términos.

triangular number A number that gives the total number of dots in a triangular pattern. The first four triangular numbers are 1, 3, 6, and 10, the numbers of dots in Figures 1 through 4 below. The *n*th triangular number can be represented by the expression $\frac{n(n+1)}{2}$. The *n*th triangular number also represents the sum of the first *n* counting numbers.

número triangular Un número que da el número total de puntos en un patrón triangular. Los primeros cuatro números triangulares son 1, 3, 6 y 10, que es el número de puntos en las Figuras 1 a 4 a continuación. El enésimo número triangular se puede representar con la expresión $\frac{n(n+1)}{2}$. El enésimo número triangular también representa la suma de los *n* primeros números para contar.

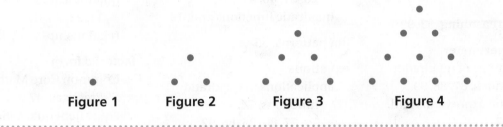

Figure 1   Figure 2   Figure 3   Figure 4

x-intercept The point where a graph crosses the *x*-axis. In the graph, the coordinates of the *x*-intercept are $(-4, 0)$.

intercepto en x El punto en el que la gráfica atraviesa el eje de las *x*. En la gráfica, las coordenadas del intercepto en *x* son $(-4, 0)$.

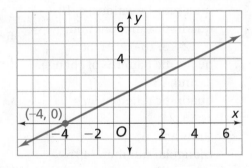

y-intercept The point where the graph crosses the *y*-axis. In a linear equation of the form $y = mx + b$, the *y*-intercept is the constant, *b*. In the graph, the coordinates of the *y*-intercept are $(0, 2)$.

intercepto en y El punto en que la gráfica atraviesa el eje de las *y*. En una ecuación lineal de la forma $y = mx + b$, el intercepto en *y* es la constante *b*. En la gráfica, las coordenadas del intercepto en *y* son $(0, 2)$.

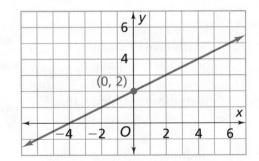

English / Spanish Glossary

Index

Acknowledgments

Cover Design

Three Communication Design, Chicago

Text

071 First paragraph of the "Did You Know" from Phytoon.com
Copyright © 2001–2002; Alinnov Science & Technology. All rights reserved.

071 Second paragraph of the "Did You Know" from Physicsweb.org
Copyright © 1996–2006 IOP Publishing Ltd. All rights reserved.

075 "Did You Know" from *The New York Times Magazine*, October 22, 1995.
Copyright © 1995 The New York Times Company.

081 Exercise 4 introduction is Copyright © 2006 The International Olympic
Committee.

Photographs

Photo locators denoted as follows: Top (T), Center (C), Bottom (B), Left (L),
Right (R), Background (Bkgd)

002 (CR) Mark Richards/PhotoEdit, (BR) F. Rauschenbach/Glow Images;
003 Radius Images/Alamy; **007** Photo Researchers, Inc.; **044** Mark Richards/
PhotoEdit; **070** Ipatov/Shutterstock; **071** Gavin Hellier/Jon Arnold Images Ltd/
Alamy; **073** F. Rauschenbach/Glow Images.